£10.41

Mastering Micros[...]

MACMILLAN MASTER SERIES

Accounting
Advanced English Language
Advanced Pure Mathematics
Arabic
Banking
Basic Management
Biology
British Politics
Business Administration
Business Communication
Business Law
C Programming
C++ Programming
Catering Theory
Chemistry
COBOL Programming
Communication
Databases
Economic and Social History
Economics
Electrical Engineering
Electronic and Electrical Calculations
Electronics
English as a Foreign Language
English Grammar
English Language
English Literature
French
French 2
German
German 2

Global Information Systems
Human Biology
Internet
Italian
Italian 2
Java
Manufacturing
Marketing
Mathematics
Mathematics for Electrical and
    Electronic Engineering
Microsoft Office
Modern British History
Modern European History
Modern World History
Pascal and Delphi Programming
Philosophy
Photography
Physics
Psychology
Science
Shakespeare
Social Welfare
Sociology
Spanish
Spanish 2
Statistics
Study Skills
Visual Basic
World Religions

Macmillan Master Series
Series Standing Order ISBN 0–333–69343–4
(outside North America only)

You can receive future titles in this series as they are published by placing a standing order.
Please contact your bookseller or, in case of difficulty, write to us at the address below with
your name and address, the title of the series and the ISBN quoted above.

Customer Services Department, Macmillan Distribution Ltd
Houndmills, Basingstoke, Hampshire RG21 6XS, England

Mastering

Microsoft® Office

Helen Holding, BSc (Hons.)
Lecturer
Department of Computer Science
University of Buckingham
Buckingham

Clare Martin, MA, MSc, DPhil
Lecturer
Department of Computer Science
University of Buckingham
Buckingham

Series Editor
William Buchanan, BSc (Hons.), CEng, PhD
Senior Lecturer
Napier University
Edinburgh

MACMILLAN

To David, Emily and Katie, and to Richard, Emma and Joe.

First published in 1998 by
MACMILLAN PRESS LTD
Houndmills, Basingstoke, Hampshire RG21 6XS
and London
Companies and representatives
throughout the world

ISBN 0–333–73059–3

A catalogue record for this book is available
from the British Library.

This book is printed on paper suitable for recycling and
made from fully managed and sustained forest sources.

10   9   8   7   6   5   4   3   2   1
07   06   05   04   03   02   01   00   99   98

Typeset by W.Buchanan in Great Britain

Printed by Biddles Ltd, Guildford and King's Lynn

Contents

Preface

This book contains a brief introduction to computers and a concise practical guide to the essential parts of Microsoft Office. It includes detailed instructions for the most recent versions of Office, but much of the text should still be relevant for older versions. The book covers four of the Office applications: Word, Excel, Access and PowerPoint. The applications need not be read sequentially, since each application is covered independently. It is necessary however, to read the chapters for each application in sequence.

The aim of the book is to leave the reader in a position where they are familiar with the fundamentals of each application and confident enough to use the on-line Help facility for any specialist problems. It can be used either as a course text or for self-paced learning by the home user or professional.

Each chapter of the book contains step-by-step instructions to take the reader through a series of connected tasks. Further exercises are included at the end of each chapter so that the skills learned in the main part of the chapter can be consolidated. This structure is particularly useful in large laboratory sessions, since it allows students to work at their own pace: faster students can move onto the extra exercises when they have finished the main body of the chapter. Each chapter is also interspersed with a number of short-answer questions to ensure that students work through the text thoroughly. It has been found in practice that each chapter takes approximately two hours, depending on the level of experience of the reader.

It is recommended that people who have no previous experience of computers use this book by first reading the introduction in Chapter 1, and then proceed to the application they are interested in: Word, Excel, Access or PowerPoint.

1 Introduction to Windows and Office

1.1 Overview

In this chapter you will learn how to do the following:

- Understand the relationship between Windows, Office, Word, Excel, Access, PowerPoint and files.
- Become familiar with the terminology used throughout this book.
- Switch on the PC and start Windows.
- Shutdown the PC.

1.2 Introduction

Microsoft Office 97 is a software package made up of several pieces of software, such as *Word* the word processor, *Excel* the spreadsheet and *PowerPoint* the graphics presentation tool. A higher specification package, called *Microsoft Office Professional 97* also includes a database called *Access*. Each of these tools or *programs* can be used alone, or in conjunction with the others. For example, you can create a spreadsheet in Excel, and insert it into a report created using Word. The instructions given in this book are written for use with *Office 97* software. In most cases, the instructions will also apply to *version 7* software, but where they differ, separate instructions identified by the ⌐⌐ label.

It is important to be able to differentiate between the *operating system,* the *package*, the *program* and the *file*. An operating system is a piece of software that acts between the person using the computer and the computer itself. In this case, the operating system is *Microsoft Windows 95*. The operating system controls how the information from the computer is displayed on the screen. In Windows 95 the information is displayed in a series of overlapping boxes, called *windows*, and functions are represented by small pictures called *icons*. The operating system also interprets the instructions of the person using the computer to tell the computer what to do. If you use the mouse to activate an icon on the screen, Windows 95 will tell the computer what that means, for

1

example, it may mean open a particular file.

The package you will use will be called either Microsoft Office 97 or Microsoft Office Professional 97, both packages are made up of a collection of tools called *programs* or *applications*. Once you have switched your computer on and the Windows 95 screen is displayed, you will need to select one of the Office programs. When you have selected which program you require, say for example Word, the screen will change and you will see the Word window on the screen.

In Word, the screen of text you will have typed is called a *document*. It is saved as a *document file* either onto a floppy disk, referred to as the *A: drive*, or onto the hard disk inside the computer, referred to as the *C: drive*. Once saved onto disk, the document can be retrieved from the disk and changed or copied any number of times. In the same way as described for Word above, Excel creates *Worksheet* files instead of document files, Access creates *Database* files and PowerPoint creates *Presentation* files.

Figure 1.1 demonstrates the relationships between the operating system, the package, the programs and the files.

This book will take you through the most useful features of Word, Excel, Access and PowerPoint. These are the features which, in our experience, are used most often and will enable you to learn in a short period of time how to produce high quality work, quickly and efficiently. Although not every possible facility and tool will be covered, you should be able to use the Help facility to find out how to use any further tools you may need.

Note: Any file names or text that you are asked to type into your document in this book is printed in bold to help the text stand out. Do not try to enter the text in bold in your documents. It should be typed in as normal, non-bold text.

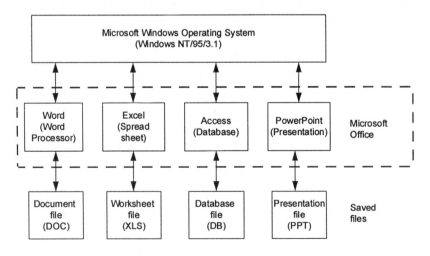

Figure 1.1 System structure

1.3 Terminology

Throughout this book, some terminology is used which you will need to be familiar with:

'Click the .... button' means that you should move the mouse so that the mouse pointer is over the requested position on the screen, then press the left-hand button on the mouse.

'Double-click...' means press the left-hand button on the mouse twice QUICKLY in succession.

'Select the ... option' means that when a list of options or menu is displayed on the screen, select the required one clicking the mouse pointer over the requested option.

'Icon' refers to a symbol or picture displayed on the screen, which when clicked on by the mouse pointer, will activate a particular function.

A *'Folder'* is the name of a location on disk where files or other folders are stored. Similar to a folder in a filing cabinet, containing many individual documents, or even other folders which themselves contain documents.

Word, Excel, Access and PowerPoint refer to Microsoft Word 97, Microsoft Excel 97, Microsoft Access 97 and Microsoft PowerPoint 97, respectively.

Windows and Office refer to Microsoft Windows 95 and either Microsoft Office 97 or Microsoft Office Professional 97.

1.4 Switching on the PC and starting Windows

The method for opening Windows will vary depending on the computer environment in which your PC is situated. You may be taken directly into the Windows screen or you may have to enter your *User name* and *Password* first. Be aware of this as you carry out the following steps to switch on the PC and start-up Windows:

1.   Make sure there are no floppy disks in the disk drives. Switch on the computer by using the button on the base unit.

2.   A Welcome to Windows screen may be displayed, asking you to enter

your **User name** and **Password**. Clicking the **Cancel** button may be the correct response, or you may need to obtain your own user name and password. You will have to find out what to do.

3.   The Windows screen will be displayed with various icons as follows:

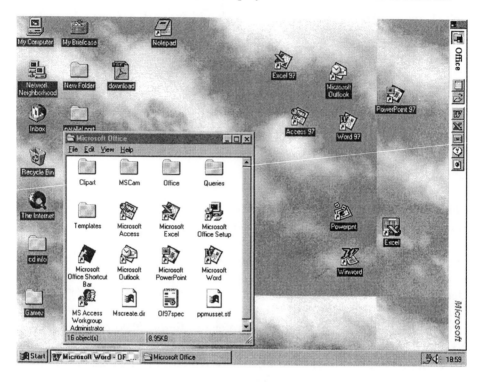

Figure 1.2 Main Windows screen

The most useful tools referred to in this book are as follows:

My Computer	**My Computer.** Clicking on this will display the files and folders (areas of storage where files can be kept) and lets you manage the files.
Recycle Bin	**Recycle Bin.** Clicking on this will display the temporary storage area that contains files deleted from the hard disk.
Start	**Start button.** Clicking on this will display the *Start Menu*. This menu offers you the facilities you will need to create, amend, run and organise your documents.

Taskbar. Whenever you start an application, such as Word or Access, an icon representing that application will appear in the taskbar. If you have more than one application open at once, and you click on the icon of the application not currently on your screen, the 'clicked on' application will be displayed as the current one on your screen. When an application is closed, its corresponding icon on the taskbar will disappear.

Note that if you are part of a network, a **Network Neighbourhood** icon may be displayed. Clicking on this will display the available resources on the network.

4.   Move the mouse such that the white arrow on the screen is over the **Start** icon. Click the left-hand button on the mouse to activate the **Start** icon.

5.   A **Start Menu** will be displayed, including the following items:

   Programs. Selecting this will display a list of application programs such as Word, Excel, Access and PowerPoint.

   Documents. Selecting this will display a list of documents you have opened recently.

   Settings. Selecting this will allow you to change the settings on your Windows screens. USE WITH CARE.

   Find. Selecting this will enable you to find a folder, file, shared computer or mail message.

   Help. Selecting this will start *Help*.

   Run. Selecting this will start a program or open a folder.

   Shut Down. Selecting this will shut down or restart your computer, or logs you off if you are using a network.

1.5 Shutting down the computer

1.   Click the **Start** icon then click on the **Shut Down** command on the *Start* window.

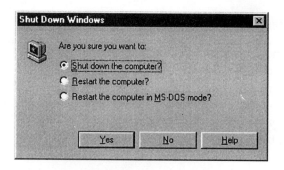

Figure 1.3 Shutdown window

2. The computer screen will ask if you are sure you want to Shut down the computer.

3. Click on **Yes**. A screen message will let you know when you can safely turn off your computer.

4. Turn your computer off at the base unit if it doesn't switch itself off automatically, and remove your floppy disk.

Before shutting down the computer, it is very important to shut down all your open windows. Remember that all open windows are represented by buttons on the taskbar. In this case, the taskbar should be empty. If it were not, you would need to restore and close each window before shutting the computer down.

2 | Microsoft Word – Getting Started

2.1 Overview

In this chapter, you will learn how to do the following:

- Start Word.
- Understand and use the Word screen.
- Use the Help feature.
- Create a document.
- Move around a document.
- Insert, delete and replace text.
- Save and retrieve a document.
- Close a document and exit from Word.

2.2 Introduction

You may have used a typewriter before. A typewriter transfers the keyed characters you depress directly onto the printed page. What you key is what you print. Any minor mistakes such as misspellings or typing errors can be corrected, if spotted quickly, using corrector ribbon or fluid, but major errors such as missing words or sentences will require the document to be re-typed.

A word processor introduces the idea of a 'virtual' or temporary document, whereby you type the document, not directly onto paper, but into the computer's memory, also called the temporary store. The typed document will also appear on the screen. In this way, the document can easily be altered and formatted. Once you are happy with the finished document, you can print it onto paper and store it as a file onto either the computer's hard disk or a floppy disk to take away with you. Once saved onto disk, the document can be changed, re-saved and printed any number of times.

Most word processors on the market today offer the same basic functionality, although the tools and facilities for carrying out these functions will vary. Word processors enable the text in a document to be formatted to enhance its appearance and layout. General layout features such as headers, footers and page numbers can also be added to the document. There are tools to enable text to be moved and copied to different positions in the document, as well as from one document to another. Word processors also enable the whole document or a specific range of pages to be printed on request. Several copies of the document can be printed at once.

Microsoft Word is a Windows-based word processor and is undeniably one of the best and most widely used on the market. A Windows-based product will offer the facilities of Windows, such as overlapping screens of information and the ability to use a mouse to click on icons or menu names on the screen, which themselves carry out functions or display pull-down menus of other functions.

The next three chapters will take you through the most useful features of Word. These are the features which, in our experience, are used most often and will enable you to produce documents of high quality quickly and efficiently. Although not every possible facility and tool will be covered, you should be able to use the Help facility to find out how to use any further tools you may need.

2.3   Starting Word and understanding the Word screen

The following steps explain how to start Word and describe the main features of the Word screen:

1.   Click the **Start** icon from the main Windows screen. Move the mouse pointer to point to, not click on, the **Programs** icon. A list of available programs will be displayed.

2.   Click on **Microsoft Word.** The Word screen with an empty document will be displayed as in Figure 2.1. The various parts of the screen are described below.

Minimise Button. If the **Application Minimise Button** is clicked, the Word window will disappear and appear as an icon on the taskbar. Click on that icon to restore the Word window. If the **Document Minimise Button** is clicked, the current document will disappear and appear as an icon above the taskbar on the initial Word window.

Restore Button. Click the **Restore button** on the minimised document's icon to restore the document to the screen.

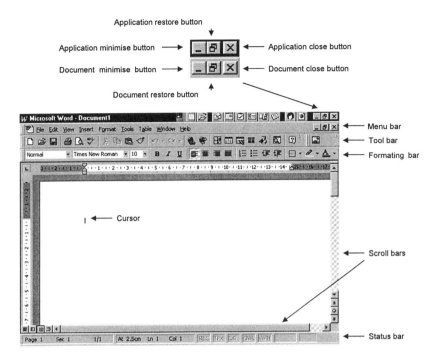

Figure 2.1 Word screen

X **Close Button.** When the **Application Close Button** is clicked, the Word window will disappear from both the screen and the taskbar. When the **Document Close Button** is clicked, only the current document will disappear. You will remain in Word.

Menu Bar. When you click one of the menu commands, a pull-down menu will be displayed.

Q1.   *Write four of the menu options available in the Menu Bar.*

Tool Bar. This bar contains icons representing the most commonly used menu functions in Word.

Q2.   *Use the mouse pointer to point at each icon in the toolbar in turn to see a short description appear underneath each. Draw the following icons: New, Open, Save, Print, Cut, Copy, Paste and Undo.*

Formatting Bar. This bar contains boxes and icons to enable you to format your text. The icons will be highlighted to show which are active for the current text.

Q3. Using the mouse pointer, click the down scroll arrow on each of the Style, Font and Font Size boxes to view the pull-down list for each. Write down the top three entries in each list.

Cursor. This flashing bold vertical line shows the position on the screen where text will be inserted when you start to type.

Scroll Bars. Dragging the grey box or clicking on the scroll arrows allows you to control which area of your document is in view.

Status Bar. This shows information about the position of the cursor in the document including page, line and column number.

Note: If your main windows screen contains a Word shortcut icon ( ), you can simply double-click on it to start Word. Refer to Figure 1.2 in Chapter 1.

2.4   Using help

Microsoft *Help* is made up of a series of screens which tell you in step-by-step detail how to use each function. The Help facility provides you with several tools which help you to find the Help screens you require.

1.   Click the **Help** option on the menu bar.

Version 7   If you are using Word 7, skip steps 2–6 below and follow the Version 7 instructions provided after step 6.

2.   Six Help options will be displayed. The three most useful are:

• **Microsoft Word Help.** The main Help screen used in Word. This facility is also available via the icon on the toolbar.
• **Contents and Index.** This Help facility enables you to browse through available Help topics or to select a particular Help topic.
• **What's This?** When this icon is clicked, a large bold '?' will appear next to the mouse pointer. Position the mouse pointer above whatever you wish to find Help about on the screen and click to see a small Help window. Click anywhere on the screen to remove it.

3.   Click the **Microsoft Word Help** option.

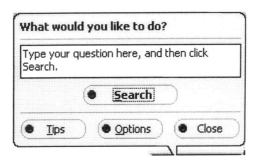

Figure 2.2 Microsoft Word Help

4. Under the box marked **What would you like to do?** type **headers and footers**, then click the **Search** box.

5. A list of associated topics will be displayed. If you do not want any of the options shown, you would type in a different title and click **Search** again. In this case, click on the **Create headers and footers** option and the appropriate Help screen will be shown.

6. Click the **Close** icon on the Help window. A small Help window will remain. If you click on it, the Microsoft Word Help window will appear. In this case, click the **Close** icon on the Help window.

Note: In all functions, clicking the **Close** or **Cancel** option or the **Close** icon will always quit you out.

Version 7 begin

2. Five Help options are listed. The two most useful are **Microsoft Word Help Topics,** which contains the Contents and Index Help tools which work in the same way as those of the same name in Office 97, and the **Answer Wizard**, which works in a similar way to the Microsoft Word Help in Office 97.

3. Click the **Answer Wizard** option.

4. Under the box marked as **1. Type your request, and then click Search**, type the following: **Create headers and footers,** then as instructed, click the **Search** box.

5. A list of associated topics will be displayed. Click on **Create headers and footers,** then click on **Display**. The Help screen for Create headers and footers will be shown.

6.   Click on **Help Topics** to get back to the previous Help screen, then click **Cancel** to get out of Help.

Version 7 end

Q4.   *Follow steps 1 to 5 to use the Microsoft Word Help to find the Help screen for the function* **Indent Paragraphs**. *Write down the first sentence of the* **Indent Paragraphs** *Help screen.*

| 2.5   Creating a document |

When you first go into Word, a blank document called **Document1** is displayed on the screen. This is called the *default* document and until you save it, it is only stored in temporary memory. You will save it later.

Q5.   *If, before you saved Document1, you created another new document, what would be the default name of the new document?*

1.   Type the following report title at the top of your document:

Using Word Wrap and the Enter Key

2.   Press the **Enter** key twice on the keyboard to get a new line and a blank line. This is the large ⏎ key to the right of the main key group.

3.   The text in the following two paragraphs must be typed continuously, without pressing the **Enter** key at the end of each line. As you reach the end of a line, Word will automatically position the text on the next line. This is called *Word Wrap*. At the end of the first paragraph, press **Enter** twice to end the paragraph and to leave a blank line before starting the second paragraph.

If you see a red wavy line appear under some words, it is the Word spelling checker telling you that it does not recognise a word. Correct the word and the line will disappear. A green wavy line is a grammar checker and may appear if you have Word 97 and have left too many spaces between words or sentences. Also note that the text on your screen will not be aligned in the same way as the text in this book. Type the following:

One of the basic features of most word processing packages on the market today is the ability to allow the person typing the text

to type continuously without pressing **Enter** at the end of each line. The word processor will position the cursor at the start of the next line. This not only means that it is faster to type the text in, but the main advantage is that if any text is removed or inserted, the word processor will automatically re-wrap the text to fill the lines.

If you wish to start a new paragraph or leave a blank line, you will need to press the **Enter** key on the keyboard.

2.6 Moving around the document

There are several methods of moving around your document. To move the cursor to a particular position on the screen, use the mouse as follows:

1. Try moving the mouse pointer around your document and click when you wish to set the cursor to the position of the pointer.

The scroll bar, shown previously in Figure 2.1, is used to view a different part of your document on the screen. You can then use the mouse to position the cursor.

2. Click the **single down arrow** ▼ on the scroll bar. The window on your screen moves 'down' your document one line at a time.

3. Click on the **grey box** between the two scroll arrows and *drag* it upwards. The view of your document will move upwards.

4. Click the **single down arrow** a few times, then click the **single up arrow** ▲ on the scroll bar to return to the top of your document once again.

When you only have a few pages of text, it may be quicker to use the scroll arrows to move around. However, if you wanted to move to the middle of a 25 page document, for example, it would be quicker to use the grey scroll box.

It is also possible to use the arrow keys and the Page up and Page down keys on the keyboard to move around the document. These keys can also be used whilst holding the control key down for a different effect. These are not covered in any detail in this book.

2.7 Inserting, deleting and replacing text

Carry out the following steps to insert new text into your document:

1. Position the cursor to the right of the words **One of the basic features of most**, then press the **space bar** on the keyboard once and type the words **of the**.

2. In the same way, insert the word **automatically** after the words **The word processor will**.

Carry out the following deletions and replacements:

3. Position the cursor to the right of the words **without pressing Enter at the end of each** and press the **backspace** key (← BkSp) repeatedly until the word **each** is deleted. The backspace key is the left facing arrow above the enter key. Then type the word **every**.

4. In the same way, delete the words **will need to** in the last paragraph, and replace them with the word **must**.

Your screen should look similar to Figure 2.3, although the layout of your paragraphs may appear slightly different.

Text can also be deleted by selecting the block of text to be deleted and then pressing the delete key. This method will be covered in the next chapter.

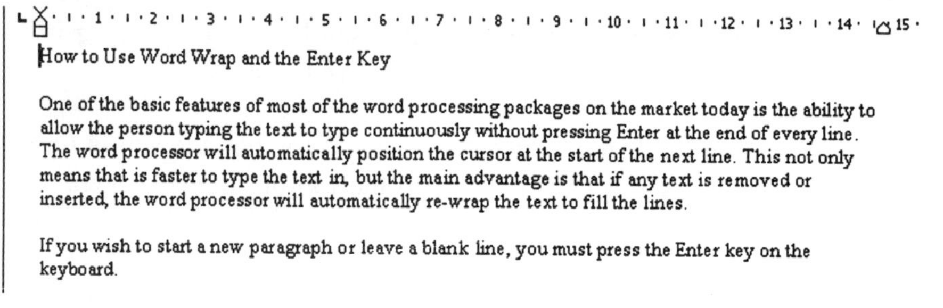

L ⋈ · ı · 1 · ı · 2 · ı · 3 · ı · 4 · ı · 5 · ı · 6 · ı · 7 · ı · 8 · ı · 9 · ı · 10 · ı · 11 · ı · 12 · ı · 13 · ı · 14 · ⊿ 15 ·

How to Use Word Wrap and the Enter Key

One of the basic features of most of the word processing packages on the market today is the ability to allow the person typing the text to type continuously without pressing Enter at the end of every line. The word processor will automatically position the cursor at the start of the next line. This not only means that is faster to type the text in, but the main advantage is that if any text is removed or inserted, the word processor will automatically re-wrap the text to fill the lines.

If you wish to start a new paragraph or leave a blank line, you must press the Enter key on the keyboard.

Figure 2.3 Written text

2.8 Saving a document

When you save a document, the computer takes the document from temporary memory and stores it as a file on disk. It is very important to save your work frequently since, until you save a document, any changes you make will be lost if the computer is switched off or if you unintentionally close your document without requesting to save it.

When you save a document, you must specify where you wish the file to be stored, either onto the hard disk inside the computer or onto a floppy disk. This book will instruct you to save your files onto a floppy disk.

1. Insert your floppy disk into the base unit and click on **File** on the menu bar, then on **Save** on the pull-down menu. The following **Save As** screen will be displayed in Figure 2.4.

    If your window displays different locations to Figure 2.4, keep clicking the **Up One Level** icon (⬆), until **My Computer** (🖳 My Computer) is shown in the **Save In** box.

2. Click **3½ Floppy (A:)** shown in the large box, then click **Open**.

3. The name displayed in the **File name** box is a *default* name made up from the first line of text from your document. Position the cursor at the end of the default file name and use the **backspace** key to delete the default name, then type **Wordwp1**, the new file name.

4. Click the **Save** box and watch the *egg timer* icon appear whilst the file is being saved. Your document will be saved under the name **Wordwp1.doc**. All Word files are saved with the **.doc** suffix, although in Windows, you are not usually shown the suffix.

Note that instead of clicking on **File** and then **Save** to get the Save window, you could have just clicked the **Save** icon on the toolbar (💾).

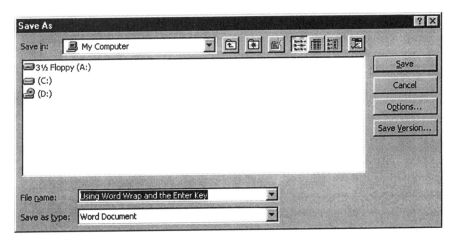

Figure 2.4 Save As window

2.9 Closing a document

Closing a document simply removes it from the computer's temporary store.

Q6.   What will happen to any changes you make to a document if you Close it before Saving the document ?

Word always gives you the chance to save any changes made to a document before closing it. To illustrate how this works, carry out the following steps:

1.   Change the word **Using** in the title line, to **How to use**. Then try to close the current document by clicking **File**, then **Close** (C̲lose).

Q7.   What happened and why?

2.   Click on **Yes**. **Wordwp1** will disappear and the empty Word screen will be displayed.

Instead of clicking **File**, then **Close**, you could have just clicked the **Close** icon on the document's window.

   It is good practice to close each document before opening or creating the next one, unless you intend to use two or more documents to work from at one time. The minimise and restore buttons would help you do this.

2.10 Retrieving a document and exiting from Word

When you retrieve a document from disk, you put a copy of it into temporary store in the computer. It can then be changed and saved again, or may simply be read or copied from before closing it without saving.

1.   Click **File**, then **Open** (☞ O̲pen...). The Open window will be displayed as in Figure 2.5.

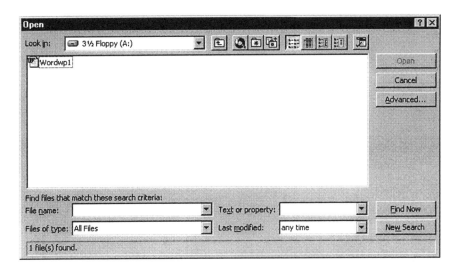

Figure 2.5 Open Window

2. In the **Look in** box, **3½ Floppy (A:)** should already be displayed. If not, click the scroll arrow and then click on **3½ Floppy (A:).** Click on **Wordwp1,** then click **Open.** The **Wordwp1** file will then be displayed on your screen.

Instead of clicking **File**, then **Open**, you could have just clicked on the **Open** icon in the tool bar (📂).

Since you have made no changes to **Wordwp1,** there is no need to save it.

3. Instead of using the **File** command, click the **Document Close** icon (❌) on the top right of the document. Make sure you do not click the **Word Close** icon on the top right corner of the screen, otherwise you will close the Word application as well as your document.

Since you have closed your document, you can now exit from Word. You may then wish to shut down the computer.

4. Click **File**, then **Exit** (E⨯it). Word will close, taking you back to the Windows main screen. Alternatively, you could have clicked the **Application Close** icon (❌) in the top right corner of the screen.

5. Click the **Start** icon then click on the **Shut Down** command on the *Start* window. The computer screen will ask if you sure you want to Shut down the computer. Click on **Yes**. A screen message will let you know when you can safely turn off your computer.

6. Turn your computer off at the base unit if it doesn't switch itself off automatically, and remove your floppy disk.

2.11 Summary

In this chapter, you will have been shown how to do the following:

- Start Word using the **Start** icon, the **Programs** and **Word** commands.
- Recognise features of the Word screen, including the menu bar, tool bar and formatting bar.
- Use **Microsoft Word Help** to find the Help screen for a function.
- Create a new document and type text into a document.
- Move around a document using both the mouse button and the scroll bar.
- Insert, delete and replace text using the mouse cursor and the delete key.
- Save and retrieve a document using the **File** then the **Save** and **Open** commands from the menu bar.
- Close a document and exit from Word using the **Close** icons on the screen.

2.12 Written exercises

2.12.1   Write down simple, step-by-step instructions, assuming you are starting from the main Windows screen, to enable someone to use Word to create a document called **Wordinv1,** stored on floppy disk, containing the following text:

You are invited to celebrate the 21st Birthday of Gina Bernof, at 15 The Grange, Marshton on Saturday 15th May from 8.00 p.m.

2.12.2   Write down instructions to enable someone to retrieve file **Wordinv1** and modify it to replace the words **You are invited**, with the words **Mr and Mrs Kevin Bernof invite you.** Insert the words **their daughter** in front of the name **Gina**. The document should be saved again, then the document and Word should be closed.

2.13.1   Create a new document called **Wordadv1**, saved onto your floppy disk, and type in the following advertisement for a personal computer:

For Sale. Personal Computer with the latest state of the art 233 MHz Microprocessor technology, high performance chipset motherboard, 32 MB RAM (expandable to 256MB), 512 Pipeline Burst Cache, 6 speed CD ROM, 14" SVGA Colour monitor, 1 MB 64-bit PCI VGA Card and full tower case with 5 5.25" disk drives. £1500. Telephone 01281 - 2578 8888 after 6 p.m.

After saving and closing the new document, retrieve it again and make the following changes:

(a)   Change the price being asked to **£999**.
(b)   Insert the text (4 PCI, 4 ISA slots, 1 shared) after the word motherboard.
(c)   Remove the text 512 Pipeline Burst Cache.

2.13.2   The following paragraph describes the fictional Italian town of Elenia in a tourist guide to Italy:

ELENIA

A pretty fishing port with a picturesque old town surrounded by hilly woodland. There is a small beach of fine, volcanic sand and a lively atmosphere in the village square. There are several local restaurants and bars and a maze of back alleys offering a wonderful range of goods from fruit and vegetables to designer clothing. There are many well hidden churches, villas and palaces to be found around the outskirts of the town. The sleepy villages of Coragio and Tarola are within an hour journey from here.

Create a new document on your floppy disk describing your home town as if it were to be included in a holiday guide.

2.13.3   Use the **Microsoft Word Help** facility to find the Help screen to tell you how to insert a footnote. Write down the four steps that the Help screen provides and amend the town description document written in

3 Microsoft Word – More Fundamentals and Printing

3.1 Overview

In this chapter, you will learn how to do the following:

- Copy your document.
- Select a block of text in a document.
- Copy, Move and Delete blocks of text.
- Undo and Redo commands.
- Use the Spelling Tool.
- Insert a Page Break.
- Preview your document.
- Print your document.
- Use different screen displays.

3.2 Introduction

By now, you will have learned how to create and retrieve a document, enter text, save and close a document. With these basic skills you could create most types of document. However, to use Word to help you to create documents quickly and efficiently, there are several other useful tools worth familiarising yourself with.

If, for example, you want to reposition a whole paragraph of text in your document, instead of deleting and retyping it, you can simply select the paragraph and move it. Another useful tool is the ability to *undo* unwanted actions. For example, if you delete a sentence, and then wish you hadn't, Word lets you *undo* the deletion so that the deleted sentence reappears. You can also use the built in dictionary in Word to check your spelling.

As well as looking at these tools which help you to create your document, you will need to able to print your document. Word offers many different options for printing a document, such as the number of copies and the range of pages to be printed. Word also provides a method of seeing what your printed document will look like on the screen before you print it.

You will have already created a document called **Wordwp1** in the previous chapter, and you will use that document to work from in this chapter. However, instead of changing the original **Wordwp1** document, you will take a copy of it and work from the new version. This useful technique will be illustrated in the following section.

3.3 Copying a document

When you retrieve a document, change it and then save it again, the changed version will overwrite the previous version saved on disk. If you want to keep the previous version of a document, you must copy your original document under a new name and then edit the new version. This can be done using the *Save As* command as follows:

1. Start **Word** then insert your floppy disk into the disk drive and retrieve the document **Wordwp1** from your floppy disk.

2. Click **File**, then click **Save As...** The same screen will be displayed as when you first save a document. Refer to Figure 3.1.

3. Change the file name from **Wordwp1** to **Wordwp2** and click the **Save** box. There are now two identical copies of this document on disk, **Wordwp1** and **Wordwp2**. **Wordwp2** is the document currently displayed on the screen.

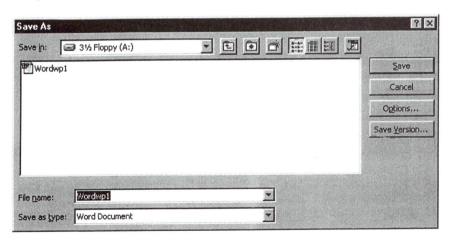

Figure 3.1 Save As window

Microsoft Word – More fundamentals and printing 21

3.4 Selecting text

In Word, it is possible to copy, move and delete a whole area or *block* of text rather than just individual characters. To do this, you must first tell the computer which *block* of text you wish to use by highlighting or *selecting* the text. There are several ways to select text in Word. The most useful method is to use the mouse pointer to highlight the text directly as follows:

1.   Position the mouse pointer to the left of the words **The word processor will automatically**, then, whilst holding down the left mouse button, *drag* the mouse to the right until the words **The word processor will automatically** are highlighted. Refer to Figure 3.2. Release the mouse button.

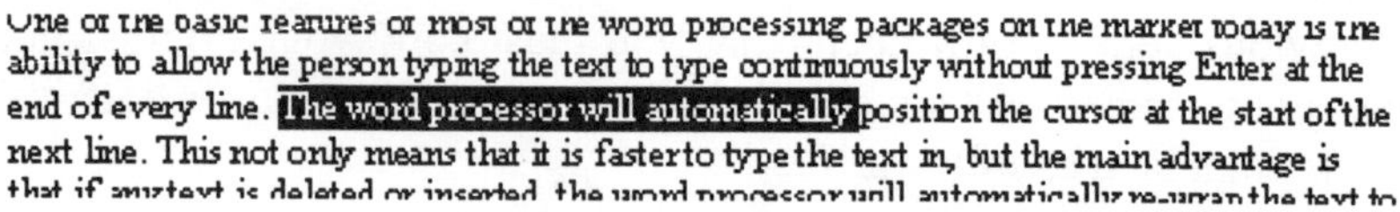

> One of the basic features of most of the word processing packages on the market today is the ability to allow the person typing the text to type continuously without pressing Enter at the end of every line. The word processor will automatically position the cursor at the start of the next line. This not only means that it is faster to type the text in, but the main advantage is that if anytext is deleted or inserted, the word processor will automatically re-wrap the text to

Figure 3.2 Selected text

2.   Click the cursor anywhere on the screen to remove the selection.

3.   This time, select the first sentence by selecting the first line then, keeping the mouse button depressed, move the mouse down to highlight the next line. You can then move the mouse further down or to the left or right if needed.

Two other methods of selecting text are illustrated as follows:

4.   Select the word **position** in the second sentence by **double-clicking** anywhere on that word. The double-clicking must be fast.

5.   Select the first four lines of the first paragraph by **clicking** to the left of the top line, and **dragging the mouse down** until the four lines are highlighted.

*Q1.   How can you select all the text in your document using the menu bar commands? [Hint: click the **Edit** menu command, then...]*

3.5 Copying blocks of text

To copy a block of text, you must first select the text, then *Copy* the text into an area in the computer's memory called the *Clipboard*. You then place the cursor where you want the copied text to be inserted, and finally insert or *Paste* a copy of the text from the clipboard into your document. Copy the first paragraph in your document to the end of your document using the menu bar:

1.   Select the whole of the first paragraph, then click the **Edit** command in the menu bar, then click **Copy.** Nothing will happen on the screen.

2.   Position the mouse cursor at the end of the last paragraph and press the **Enter** key twice. Click the **Edit** command.

Q2.   *Try to click the **Cut** and **Copy** commands. What has happened to them and why?*

3.   Click Paste.

Since text remains in the clipboard until it is overwritten by further text being placed in the clipboard or until Word is closed, it is possible to paste text many times. Try copying the title line twice using the icons as follows:

4.   Select the title line, then click the **Copy** icon .

5.   Position the cursor at the end of the title line and press the **Enter** key once only to get a new line, then click the **Paste** icon to insert the copy of the title line into the document.

6.   If your cursor is currently at the end of the new title, press the **Enter** key once again to get a new line.

7.   Click the **Paste** icon again. A second copy of the title line should be inserted. Your document should now look similar to Figure 3.3.

Using Word Wrap and the Enter Key
Using Word Wrap and the Enter Key
Using Word Wrap and the Enter Key

One of the basic features of most of the word processing packages on the market today is the ability to allow the person typing the text to type continuously without pressing Enter at the end of every line. The word processor will automatically position the cursor at the start of the next line. This not only means that it is faster to type the text in, but the main advantage is that if any text is deleted or inserted, the word processor will automatically re-wrap the text to fill the lines.

If you wish to start a new paragraph or leave a blank line, you must press the Enter key on the keyboard.

One of the basic features of most of the word processing packages on the market today is the ability to allow the person typing the text to type continuously without pressing Enter at the end of every line. The word processor will automatically position the cursor at the start of the next line. This not only means that it is faster to type the text in, but the main advantage is that if any text is deleted or inserted, the word processor will automatically re-wrap the text to fill the lines.

Figure 3.3 Wordwp2 with pasted paragraph and title lines

3.6   Moving blocks of text

To move a block of text, you do the same as when you copy text, except that text is not *copied* to the clipboard, it is *cut* to the clipboard. This means that it is removed from the document and stored in the clipboard until you paste it back into the document. Move the second paragraph to the bottom of your document as follows:

1.   Select the whole of the second paragraph, starting **If you wish to ...**

2.   Click the **Edit** command in the menu bar, then click **Cut**. The selected paragraph will disappear from the screen.

3.   Position the cursor at the end of the last paragraph in your document and press the **enter** key twice, then click the **Paste** icon.

Move the second title line to below the first paragraph using the icons:

4.   Select the second title line, then click the **Cut** icon ✂.

5.   Position the cursor at the start of the blank line above the second paragraph, then click the **Paste** icon to insert the title line.

Your document should look similar to Figure 3.4.

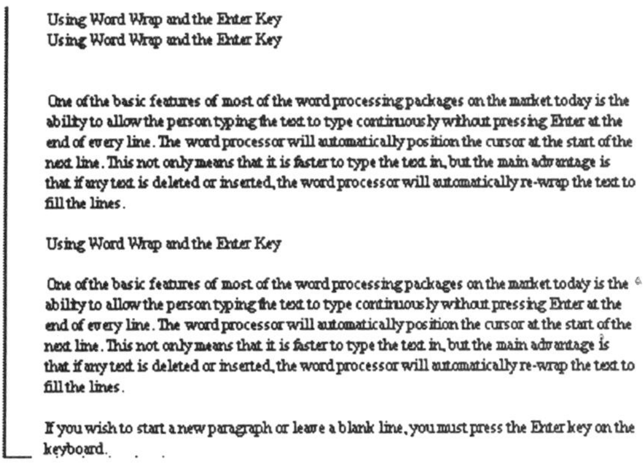

Using Word Wrap and the Enter Key
Using Word Wrap and the Enter Key

One of the basic features of most of the word processing packages on the market today is the ability to allow the person typing the text to type continuously without pressing Enter at the end of every line. The word processor will automatically position the cursor at the start of the next line. This not only means that it is faster to type the text in, but the main advantage is that if any text is deleted or inserted, the word processor will automatically re-wrap the text to fill the lines.

Using Word Wrap and the Enter Key

One of the basic features of most of the word processing packages on the market today is the ability to allow the person typing the text to type continuously without pressing Enter at the end of every line. The word processor will automatically position the cursor at the start of the next line. This not only means that it is faster to type the text in, but the main advantage is that if any text is deleted or inserted, the word processor will automatically re-wrap the text to fill the lines.

If you wish to start a new paragraph or leave a blank line, you must press the Enter key on the keyboard.

Figure 3.4 Wordwp2 with moved title line and second paragraph

3.7 Deleting blocks of text

To delete text from a document, you must first select the text, then either *delete* it using the backspace or delete keys or the clear command using the menu bar. Carry out both types of deletion as follows:

1. Select the top title line, then press the **Backspace** key (← BkSp). If you are left with a blank line at the top of the document, press the key marked **Delete** on the keyboard to remove it.

2. Select, in one block, the first paragraph and the title line below it. Click the **Edit** command on the menu bar and click **Clear**. Your document should now look similar to Figure 3.5.

3. Click the **Save** icon to save the document, **Wordwp2**.

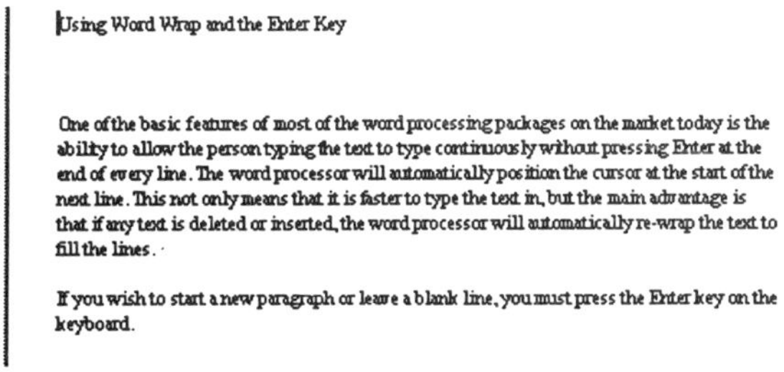

Using Word Wrap and the Enter Key

One of the basic features of most of the word processing packages on the market today is the ability to allow the person typing the text to type continuously without pressing Enter at the end of every line. The word processor will automatically position the cursor at the start of the next line. This not only means that it is faster to type the text in, but the main advantage is that if any text is deleted or inserted, the word processor will automatically re-wrap the text to fill the lines.

If you wish to start a new paragraph or leave a blank line, you must press the Enter key on the keyboard.

Figure 3.5 Wordwp2 with deleted title line and deleted paragraphs

3.8 Undo command

A very useful feature of Word is the ability to reverse or *undo* actions that have just been carried out. For example, if you deleted a word or block of text and then decided it should not have been deleted, you could *undo* the deletion and the text would re-appear.

1. Delete the title line in your document using the **Edit, Clear** method described in the previous section.

2. Click on the **Edit** command on the menu bar, then click **Undo Clear**. The deleted text should reappear.

You can also undo newly typed text or changes made in the same way:

3. Place your cursor anywhere on your document and type the words **undo this.**

4. Click the **Undo** icon . The words **undo this** should disappear.

It is also possible to re-apply or *redo* a reversed action carried out by an *undo*.

5. Click the **Redo** icon . The words **undo this** should reappear.

You can undo more than one action at once, by clicking the **down arrow** next to the **undo icon** to view a list of previous actions, then selecting those you wish to undo. You can redo more than one undone action in the same way.

6. Close the document without saving the undo and redo changes, by clicking the **Document Close** icon. When asked if you wish to save the changes to **Wordwp2**, click **No**. Stay in Word.

3.9 Using the spelling tool

A useful feature of Word is a tool that automatically compares the words in your document against a dictionary of words held in the computer's memory. Any unrecognised or repeated words are underlined in red. If the word is misspelled, you can either correct the word yourself or let Word help you with suggested spellings. If the word is a colloquialism or scientific terminology, for example, you could tell Word to ignore it or add it to its dictionary.

1. Create a new document by clicking the **New** icon on the toolbar.

2. Type the following text, exactly as printed on this page. Red wavy lines should appear under the underlined words as shown below:

These days, it is <u>expeced</u> that any document produced using a word processor should have been automatically checked for spelling mistakes. Most words not recognised by the Word dictionary will need to be <u>be</u> corrected, with the exception of technical terms and <u>collogiulisms</u>, such as the quote "I'll give you a <u>tenner</u> for it and no more than a <u>tenner</u>".

---

3. Position the mouse cursor on each underlined word in turn, then click the **right mouse button**. A small window will appear on the screen. The top section may list suggested spellings of the word and under that will be listed possible actions you can take, such as *Ignore All* and *Add*. Carry out the following actions for each underlined word:

    <u>Expeced</u>. Select the word **expected** in the list and click the **left mouse button**.

Q3. *What happens to the text ?*

    <u>Be</u>. Click the option **Delete Repeated Word**.

    <u>Collogiulisms</u>. Select the word **colloquialisms** and click the **left mouse button**.

    <u>Tenner</u>. This word is correctly spelled but is a colloquialism and therefore not in the dictionary. In this instance do not add it to the dictionary, just click **Ignore All**.

Q4. *What has happened to the red-underlined word tenner at the end of the paragraph and why?*

Although you would usually correct your misspellings as you type, by clicking the **Spelling and Grammar** icon , Word will search through your document and help you correct any remaining words underlined in red. Word 97 can also check your grammar, underlining any grammatical errors or incorrect numbers of spaces in a green wavy line.

4. **Save** your new document onto your floppy disk under the file name **Wordsp1**. Then **Close** the document, but stay in Word.

5. Retrieve the document **Wordwp1** from your floppy disk.

6. Click **File**, then click **Save As...** and change the file name from **Wordwp1** to **Wordwp3**. Click the **Save** box.

3.10 Inserting a page break

Normally when you are typing and you reach the end of a page, Word will automatically throw a new page for you. However, to insert a page at any position in your document, do the following:

1. Position the cursor where you wish the page break to be inserted. In this case, at the start of the second paragraph. Click **Insert** on the menu bar, then click **Break**. The **Page Break** option will already be selected, so just click **OK**.

Q5. What would the top of the new page look like if you had positioned the cursor on the blank line above the second paragraph?

2. Save the changed document **Wordwp3** by clicking the **Save** icon.

3.11 Preview your document

Word provides you with a tool to enable you to see a miniature version of what your document will look like when it is printed.

1. Click the **File** on the menu bar, then click **Print Preview**. A miniature version of **Wordwp3** will be displayed. The number of pages shown on the screen may vary. Refer to Figure 3.6.

2. If only one page is on your screen, click the **Multiple Pages** icon , then click one of the pages in the small **Multiple Pages** window.

3. If both pages are on your screen, click the **One Page** icon , then click the **double scroll arrows** on the scroll bar to view each page.

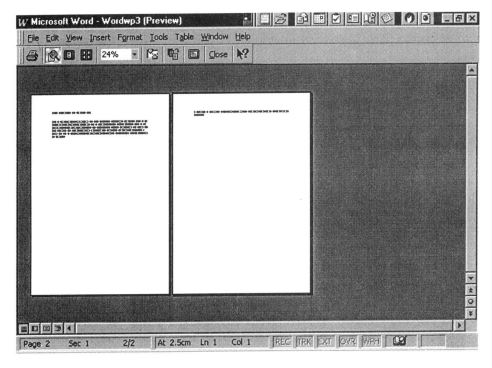

Figure 3.6 Print Preview of both pages of Wordwp3

4.   Click the box with the word **Close.**

Instead of using the **File** and **Print Preview** menu commands, you could click the **Print Preview** icon on the tool bar 🔍.

3.12 Print your document

Printing a document in Word is very straightforward and flexible. You can either click the print icon, which will print one copy of the whole document, the default, or you can use the Print command, which will allow you to request various printing options.

When you request a print, the request will be stored in a *print queue*. When your request reaches the head of queue, your document will be printed. If there is a printing problem, such as no paper in the printer, a message will appear on your screen. You will be asked if you wish Word to *Retry* your print request on the printer or *Cancel* your print request from the queue. *Cancelling* is often the safest option. You can then sort out the problem and then re-request your print.

1.   Print one copy of your two page **Wordwp3** document by clicking the **Print** icon ![printer icon] on the toolbar.

This time you are going to request two copies of the first page of your document using the print menu commands as follows:

2.   Click the **File** command on the menu bar, then click **Print**. The following screen will be displayed. Your printer details may differ (Figure 3.7).

There are three main sections in the Print window:

- **Printer** provides details about the printer you are using. It is not wise to change these unless you are familiar with the printer set-up.
- **Page Range** allows you to select whether you wish to print all the pages in your document, the current page displayed on the screen, or a specific page or range of pages, such as 4 or 1, 2, 3 or 1–6.
- **Copies** allows you enter how many copies of the print you require.

Note that clicking the **Options** box allows you to request other settings, such as reverse order printing, which is useful for some ink jet printers.

3.   Click on the white circle next to the word **Pages** in the **Page range** section, then type a **1** in the **Pages** box.

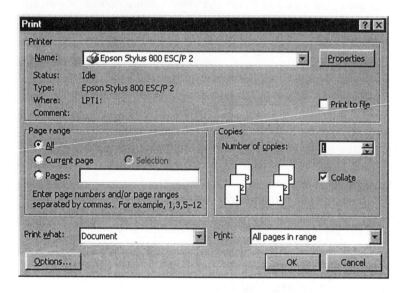

Figure 3.7 Print window

4. Click on the **up arrow** in the **Number of copies** box to get the number 2 to appear in the box, then click on the **OK** box.

3.13 Using different screen displays

There are several ways to view a document in Word. You are probably using the *Normal* default view currently.

1. Click on the **View** option on the menu bar. A pull-down menu of views will be displayed.

There are five main views:

- **Normal.** Displays the document in a similar format to the way it would appear when printed. Some features, such as headers, do not appear.
- **Online Layout.** Text appears larger and is wrapped to fit the window, making reading the text on screen as clear and easy as possible.
- **Page Layout.** Displays the document in exactly the same format as it will look when it is printed out.
- **Outline.** Displays only selected parts of your document and nothing else. For example, viewing only headings to help you structure your document.
- **Master Document.** This tool enables you to group and view several documents in one Master document.

If you also select **Full Screen,** the selected view will be displayed without the title, menu and tool bars, rulers and status line. Click the **Close Full Screen** icon or press the **Esc** key to return to the previous screen.

Version 7   The **Online Layout** view is not available.

2. Click on each of the views to see their effect on the screen.

3. Close your **Wordwp3** document. You should not be asked to save it since you have not made any changes to it since you saved it last. **Close** Word and **Shut Down** the computer as described in the previous chapter. Remember to remove your floppy disk.

3.14 Summary

In this chapter, you will have been shown how to do the following:

- Copy your document using the **File** and **Save As** commands.
- Select a block of text in a document using the mouse.
- Copy a block of text using the **Copy** and **Paste** commands or icons.
- Move a block of text using the **Cut** and **Paste** commands or icons.
- Delete a block of text using the **backspace key**.
- Reverse actions carried out using the **Undo** command or icon, and also to re-apply undone actions using the **Redo** icon.
- Use the **Spelling Tool** to correct misspellings.
- Insert a Page Break using the **Insert** and **Break** commands.
- **Preview** your document to see how it will look when printed.
- Print your document using the default **Print** icon and the **Print** command.
- Use different screen displays to view your document.

3.15 Written exercises

3.15.1 Write down simple, step-by-step instructions, assuming you are starting from the main Windows screen, to enable someone to use Word to create a document containing the following text:

How to Create a New Page

When you are typing text using Word and you reach the end of a page, Word automatically throws a new page for you. However, if you want to insert your own page break, do the following:

Position the cursor at the point at which you wish the new page to start.

Click the Insert command on the menu bar, then click the Break command. The Page break option will already be selected, so just click the OK box.

Your instructions should describe how to do the following tasks:

(a) Create the document, then save onto floppy disk as **Wordc3d1**.

(b)   Make a copy of the document on floppy disk called **Wordc3d2** and change the new copy as follows:

- Delete the second paragraph, then Undo the deletion
- Move the top paragraph to the bottom of the document
- Place a copy of the heading line underneath itself.

3.15.2   Write down simple, step-by-step instructions, assuming you are already in the Word screen, to enable someone to do the following:

(a)   Retrieve the four-page document **Wordc3d3** from floppy disk.

(b)   Preview the document and view each page.

(c)   Request to print three copies of pages 2 and 3 of the document.

3.16 Practical exercises

3.16.1 Create a new document on floppy disk called **Wordc3d4** with the following text:

How to Move a Block of Text

Select the text by positioning the mouse pointer to the left of the text, then dragging the mouse pointer to the right until the text is highlighted.

Then move the text into the Clipboard by clicking on the Cut icon on the toolbar. The highlighted text will disappear from the screen.

Finally, the cursor must be positioned where the text is to be moved to, then click the Paste icon on the toolbar. The text will be inserted after the cursor.

Carry out the following tasks:

(a)   Copy the second paragraph to the bottom of the document.

(b) Delete the paragraph starting **Finally, the cursor...**, then use the **Undo** icon to replace the deleted paragraph.

(c) Print two copies of the document

(d) Copy the document on floppy disk under a new name **Wordc3d5**.

(e) Create a page break at the start of the paragraph starting **Finally, the cursor must be**.

(f) Preview both pages of your document, then print one copy of page two, then one copy of both pages.

3.16.2 Create a new document called **Wordcv1** on your floppy disk and type in a brief curriculum vitae for yourself, no more than two pages in length. The main heading should be **Curriculum Vitae**, with the four sub-headings: **Personal Details, Qualifications, Work Experience** and **Additional Information**. The **Additional Information** paragraph must be written in continuous format, not in list form.

Carry out the following tasks:

(a) View the document in **Outline** and then in **Page Layout** format. End up in **Normal** view.

(b) Use the Spelling Tool for each word underlined in red.

(c) Move the **Qualifications** section such that it appears between the **Work Experience** and **Additional Information** sections.

(d) Preview your document then print one copy of it.

Microsoft Word – Text Enhancement and Document Layout

4.1 Overview

In this chapter, you will learn how to do the following:

- Change the appearance and size of text.
- Use Paragraph Styles.
- Align text to the centre, left or right of a page, or justify the text.
- Set up line spacing.
- Indent a block of text.
- Use bullet points.
- Define the page layout.
- Create headers and footers.
- Add page numbers.

4.2 Introduction

By now, you should be able to create or copy a multi-page document, edit it using the block move and copy commands and make use of several other useful tools such as the spelling checker and be able to print the document.

Word includes many tools to enhance the appearance of your document. This can be done by changing the format and alignment of the text, adding bullet points to lists, as well as by indenting text and setting up specific spaces between the lines. Word also provides tools to enable headers and footers to be set up to appear at the top and bottom of each printed page, as well as to set up page numbers throughout the document. Another important feature of Word is the Page Setup definition, which contains the layout instructions for the whole document, such as the margin sizes and whether the document is portrait or landscape, for example.

4.3   Changing the appearance and size of text

When you create a document, it is often useful to be able to change the appearance or *format* of certain areas of text, such as titles and headings. You may wish to underline some text or set text to appear in **bold** or in *italics*. You can also change the font of the lettering, as well as the size of the letters. The formatting bar will show you which format setting has been applied to the current text, as described in Chapter 2. Change the appearance of existing text in the **Wordwp1** document as follows:

1.   Start **Word** then insert your floppy disk into the disk drive and retrieve the document **Wordwp1** from your floppy disk.

2.   Click **File**, then click **Save As...** Change the file name to **Wordwp4** and click the **Save** box.

Change the format of the last paragraph to Impact font, bold and italic, with a dotted underline using the menu bar as follows:

3.   Select the last paragraph starting **If you wish ...** and click **Format** on the menu bar, then click **Font**. Refer to Figure 4.1.

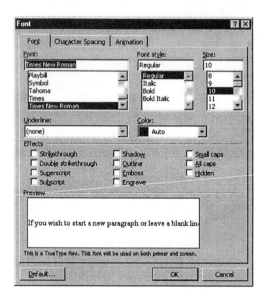

Figure 4.1 Font window

Version 7   The **Font** window will have a different layout

4. Click the **up** or **down scroll** arrows on the **Font** list to find, then click on, **Impact**. Click the **Font** style of **Italic**, then click the **down scroll arrow** on the **underline** box, currently displaying **(none)**, and click **dotted**. The **Preview** box will show you how your text will appear.

Q1.   *In the **Font** menu command box, which **Effect** box would you need to click on to set your text to capitals?*

5. Click **OK**. Click anywhere on the text to remove the highlight. Refer to Figure 4.2.

If you wish to start a new paragraph or leave a blank line, you must press the Enter key on the keyboard.

Figure 4.2 Second paragraph set to Impact, Italic with dotted underline

Unless you wish to use a specific type of underline, special effect or specific character spacing, it is much quicker to use the formatting bar icons instead of the menu commands. Refer to Figure 4.3. Change the title line as follows:

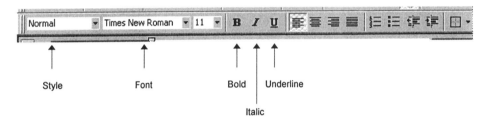

Figure 4.3 Formatting bar

6. Select the title line, then click the **down scroll arrow** to the right of the **Font** box on the formatting bar. Click **Bookman Old Style**. Leave the title line selected.

7. Click the **down scroll arrow** to the right of the **Font Size** box on the formatting bar. Click on **14**. Click on the **underline** icon **U̲**, then the **bold** icon **B** on the formatting bar. Click anywhere on the screen to de-select the text.

Instead of selecting existing text and setting the format for it, you can set up the format you require before typing the text. You must then turn off the format setting when you have finished that section of text. Type in more text:

8.   Position the cursor at the end of the first paragraph. Take a note of the current font and font size settings. Press **enter** twice then select **Courier New** font and **14** font size on the formatting bar as before and click the **italic** icon *I* .

9.   Type the following text: **This not only saves time, but also removes the risk of introducing typing errors by re-typing quantities of text.**

10. De-activate the italic setting by clicking the **italic** icon again, and then change the font and font size back to their previous settings. Refer to Figure 4.4.

How to Use Word Wrap and the Enter Key

One of the basic features of most of the word processing packages on the market today is the ability to allow the person typing the text to type continuously without pressing Enter at the end of every line. The word processor will automatically position the cursor at the start of the next line. This not only means that is faster to type the text in, but the main advantage is that if any text is removed or inserted, the word processor will automatically re-wrap the text to fill the lines.

This not only saves time, but also removes the risk of introducing typing errors by re-typing quantities of text.

If you wish to start a new paragraph or leave a blank line, you must press the Enter key on the keyboard.

Figure 4.4 Wordwp4 with different format settings

11. Click the **Save** icon to save **Wordwp4** document on your floppy disk.

4.4   Using paragraph styles

A *Style* is a complete setting of formats, including font, font size, bold, italic, and type of underline. When you create a new document, the style that is set up is the default style, *Normal*. If you do not want to use the Normal format settings, you could choose a different style, or you could set your own format settings as described in the previous section. The quickest and most consistent way to set up the format for areas of your document such as headings and sub-headings, is to use a predefined style. Try it out as follows:

1.   Place the cursor at the start of the title line, then click the **down scroll arrow** next to the **Style** box and select **Heading2**. Refer back to Figure 4.3. The title line will change to Arial font, font size 12, bold and italic. Your text should look similar to Figure 4.5

How to Use Word Wrap and the Enter Key

Figure 4.5 Title in Heading2 Style

2. Leave the cursor at the start of the first paragraph and select the **Heading1** style as above.

Q2.   What are the settings in the Formatting bar for this paragraph?

Note that Style, as well as many of the other formatting tools in this chapter, are applied automatically to a whole paragraph, which is any section of text ending when the **enter** key is pressed on the keyboard. You therefore do not need to select the paragraph, but place the cursor somewhere on the paragraph.

4.5   Aligning text

The text in a document can be aligned in one of four ways, either left, centre, right or fully justified. Refer to Figure 4.6 below:

1. Click anywhere on the heading and click **Format** on the menu bar, then click **Paragraph**. The **Indents and Spacing** window will be displayed. Refer to Figure 4.7.

Version 7   The **Paragraph** window will have a different layout

2. Click the **down scroll arrow** to the right of the **Alignment** box and click **Centred**. Watch the **Preview** change, then click **OK**.

Left aligned text is typically used in many modern computer-learning books.	Right aligned text is typically used when wrapping text round a graphic object.	Centre aligned text is typically used in on-screen presentations

Fully justified text is used in most professionally produced books, where spaces are added to the text so that the text touches both the left and right-hand sides of the document.

Figure 4.6 Alignment styles

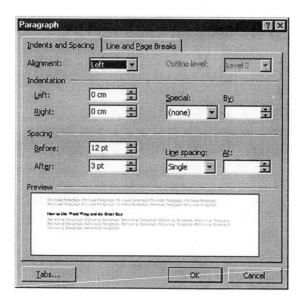

Figure 4.7 Paragraph Format window

3.   Position the cursor anywhere on the first paragraph. Click the **Align Right** icon ▤. Watch what happens, then click the **Justify** icon ▤. Refer to Figure 4.8.

How to Use Word Wrap and the Enter Key

One of the basic features of most of the word processing packages on the market today is the ability to allow the person typing the text to type continuously without pressing Enter at the end of every line. The word processor will automatically position the cursor at the start of the next line. This not only means that is faster to type the text in, but the main advantage is that if any text is removed or inserted, the word processor will automatically re-wrap the text to fill the lines.

Figure 4.8 Centre aligned headings and justified paragraph

4.6   Setting spaces between lines

Sometimes when you type a formal document for review by a third party, you are required to use 1.5 or double line width space between the lines. The **Format, Paragraph** menu command allows you to set the line spacing.

1.   Position the cursor at the start of the first paragraph and click **Format** on the menu bar, then click **Paragraph**. The **Indents and Spacing** window should be displayed.

One of the basic features of most of the word processing packages on the market today is the ability to allow the person typing the text to type continuously without pressing Enter at the end of every line. The word processor will automatically position the cursor at the start of the next line. This not only means that is faster to type the text in, but the main advantage is that if any text is removed or inserted, the word processor will automatically re-wrap the text to fill the lines.

Figure 4.9 1.5 line spacing

2. Click the **down scroll arrow** to the right of the **Line spacing** box and click **1.5 lines**. The **Preview** will show you what your paragraph will look like. Click **OK**. Refer to Figure 4.9.

4.7   Indenting a block of text

When you wish to indent a block of text, you should always use one of tools available for that task, such as the **Paragraph** command, the **Ruler** or the **Increase Indent** icon. If you create the indent yourself by inserting spaces in your text or using the tab key, you will lose the effectiveness of the word wrap utility and will have trouble amending your text. Indent text as follows:

1. With the cursor at the start of the first paragraph, click **Format** on the menu bar, then click **Paragraph**. The **Indents and Spacing** window will be displayed.

2. Use the **up scroll arrow** next to the **Left** box under the **Indentation** heading to change it to **3 cm** or **1.2 inches,** depending on the units displayed. Overwrite the zero value in the **Right** box with **2 cm** or **0.8 inches**. Watch the example change in the **Preview** box. Click **OK**.

3. With the cursor at the start of the first paragraph, click **Format**, then **Paragraph** as before.

4. Click the **down scroll arrow** on the **Special** box and click **Hanging**. Use the **up scroll arrow** next to the **By** box to change it to **1.5 cm** or **0.6 inches**. Watch the **Preview** change. Click **OK**. Your document should look similar to Figure 4.10.

5. Keep the cursor at the start of the first paragraph. There should be a ruler at the top of the document. Refer back to Figure 4.8. If not, click **View** on the menu bar, then click against **Ruler**.

How to Use Word Wrap and the Enter Key

One of the basic features of most of the word processing packages on the market today is the ability to allow the person typing the text to type continuously without pressing Enter at the end of every line. The word processor will automatically position the cursor at the start of the next line. This not only means that is faster to type the text in, but the main advantage is that if any text is removed or inserted, the word processor will automatically re-wrap the text to fill the lines.

Figure 4.10 3 cm left indentation, 2 cm right indentation, hanging by 1.5 cm

6. The **downward facing arrow** at the top left of the ruler carries out the same function as the **Left Indentation** box in the **Indents and Spacing** window. **Click** on it and **drag** it above the **5 cm** mark on the ruler, or the **2 inch** mark. When you let the mouse button go, watch the paragraph re-format.

7. The **upward facing arrow** at the bottom right of the ruler carries out the same function as the **Right Indentation** box. **Click** and **drag** it below the **11 cm** mark on the ruler, or the **4.4 inch** mark.

8. **Click** and **drag** the upward facing arrow on the bottom left of the ruler to below the **6 cm** mark on the ruler, or the **2.4 inch** mark. The ruler should look like Figure 4.11.

Q3.   *How does the upward facing arrow on the left of the ruler affect text and which box(es) does this arrow represent on the **Indents and Spacing** window?*

9. Position the cursor on the second paragraph. Click the **Increase Indent** icon ▥ three times, then click the **Decrease Indent** icon ▥ twice, to see their effect on the text.

You can either apply the indent settings to a pre-typed paragraph as above, or you can set the indent settings up and then type the text.

Figure 4.11 Ruler with indent triangles (shown in cms)

10. **Close** document **Wordwp4** without saving it but stay in Word.

4.8   Using bullet points

Word offers a range of bullet point styles to choose from, and also a bullets icon on the toolbar, which will set up whichever type of bullet was requested most recently using the menu commands. Try bullets out:

1.   Create a new document by clicking the **New** icon on the toolbar and type the following: **Office applications have several mouse pointers. Some of these are:**

2.   Press the **enter** key twice. Then click **Format** on the menu bar, then on **Bullets and Numbering**. If the **Bulleted** window is not at the front, click the **Bulleted** tab. Click on one of the **Bulleted** windows, then click **OK**.

3.   Notice that the **Bullets** icon on the toolbar is highlighted since Bullets are currently selected. Type the following, pressing the **enter** key at the end of each sentence:

The hourglass which appears when you are waiting to perform a function.

The arrow which appears when the pointer is placed over menus, scrolling bars and buttons.

The I-beam which appears in normal text areas of the screen.

4.   To stop the bullet points, press **enter** at the end of the last bullet point line. A bullet point will appear at the start of the next line. Click the **Bullets** icon, which is currently highlighted. The bullet point will disappear and you can type as usual again. Type:

This line should not be part of the bullet points.

Your document should look like Figure 4.12.

Text enhancement and document layout   43

Office applications have several mouse pointers. Some of these are:

♦ The hourglass which appears when you are waiting to perform a function.
♦ The arrow which appears when the pointer is placed over menus, scrolling bars and buttons.
♦ The I-beam which appears in normal areas of the screen.
This line should not be part of the bullet points.

Figure 4.12 Bullet points

5.   Select the three lines of bullet points together in one block and click on the highlighted **Bullets** icon on the formatting toolbar.

Q4.   What happened to the text and the icon? What happens if you click on the icon again?

Numbering is used in a similar way as bullets but is not covered in this book.

6.   Click the **Save** icon to save the document on floppy disk, entering the new file name **Wordbp1,** then click **Save.** Close Wordbp1 but stay in Word.

4.9   Defining the page layout

When you first create a document, you should always check that the *Page Setup* is correct for your document. **Page Setup** is one of the options listed under the **File** command in the menu bar.

1.   Open document **Wordwp3** from your floppy disk, which should have two pages. Click **File**, then click **Save As** to save the document on floppy disk under new name **Wordwp5.**

2.   Click on **File** on the menu bar, then click **Page Setup.**

There are four main areas of Page Setup:

- **Margins.** Defines the margin sizes for the document.
- **Paper Size.** Defines the paper sizes for the printed document. The part of this screen you may sometimes wish to change is the orientation of the document, to be either **Portrait** [ ] or **Landscape** [ ]

- **Paper Source.** This section tells the printer which paper tray to use.
- **Page Layout.** Defines where the sections will start, how the headers and footers will fit together as well as defining the vertical alignment of the top line of each page and setting line numbers.

The two most commonly used options are **Margins** and **Paper Size.**

3.   Click on the **Margins** tab if it is not displayed. Refer to Figure 4.13.

4.   Click the **up scroll arrow** on the **Top** margin box to change the top margin to **4 cm** or **1.6 inches**, then position the cursor on the **Bottom** margin box, delete the existing amount, then type **4 cm** or **1.6 inches.** Note how the **Preview** picture changes each time. Make sure you DO NOT press Enter or click OK at any point, otherwise the changes will be applied to the document.

5.   In the same way as either of the two methods above, change the **Left** margin to **1 cm** or **0.4 inches** and the **Right** margin to **1.5 cm** or **0.6 inches.**

Q5.   What effect would selecting the Mirror Margins box have?

6.   Click on **Paper Size,** then click the empty circle next to **Landscape.** Watch the **Preview** change then click against **Portrait.**

7.   Since these changes are just for practice, press **Cancel.**

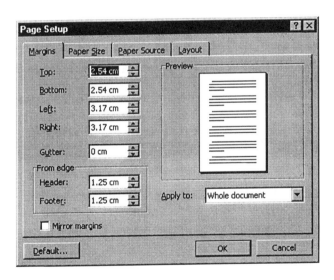

Figure 4.13 Page Setup, Margins

4.10 Creating headers and footers in Microsoft Word

A header and footer are pieces of text which appear at the top and bottom of every page. To create a header or footer, you must view your document using the View option called *Header and Footer*. Many of the views in Word do not show the headers and footers, but they will appear on the Page Layout view and when printed.

1. Click **View** on the menu bar, then click **Header and Footer**. The empty header will be displayed to you, outlined by a dotted line as well as the Header and Footer toolbar. You may need to move the toolbar to see the header by clicking the title bar on the toolbar and dragging it down the screen.

2. Type your name, followed by space, then type **A:\Wordwp5.doc** which is the full path name of the document.

3. Click on the **Switch between Header and Footer** icon 🖳. The footer will be displayed to you.

You can add page numbers in headers or footers by clicking the Page Numbers icon, but you will be creating page numbers using the **Insert, Page Numbers** commands in the next section.

4. Leave the cursor at the left of the footer, click the **Insert Date** icon 🗓, which inserts the current date held on the computer into your footer. Press the **space bar**, then click the **Insert Time** icon 🕒. This is the current time. Click on **Close** and the screen will return to how it looked before. The Header and Footer will not be shown.

5. Click **View** on the menu bar, then click **Page Layout**. Scroll up and down to see that each page has a header and a footer, both pale.

6. **Save** the document **Wordwp5** by clicking the **Save** icon.

4.11 Add page numbers in Microsoft Word

When you add page numbers to a document, you can specify where on the page you want the number to appear and whether a page number should be shown on the first page, as in the case of a title page. You can also specify which number system to use. Apply page numbers to **Wordwp5** as follows:

1.   Stay in Page layout view. Click **Insert** on the menu bar, then click **Page Numbers**. Refer to Figure 4.14.

2.   The **Position** box should display **Bottom of the Page (Footer)**. If not, click the **down scroll arrow** on the **Position** box and select it.

3.   Click the **down scroll arrow** on the **Alignment** box and select **Center.** Ensure that the selection box next to **Show Number on First Page** has been selected and has a tick in it. The **Preview** box shows you what it will look like. Click **OK** and scroll up and down to see the page numbers on each page, pale like the header and footer.

When you create a new document, it is set up as one section such that all pages are labelled as Sec 1 in the status bar at the bottom of the screen. If you wished to split your document up by chapters, such that the page numbers started at 1 at the start of each chapter, you would create a new section for each chapter. This is done using the **Insert, Break** command, referred to in Chapter 3 to create page breaks.

4.   **Save** then **Close** document **Wordwp5**, then **Close** Word and shut down the computer.

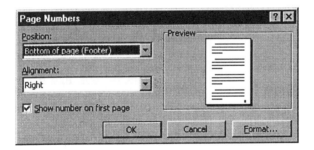

Figure 4.14 Insert, Page Numbers

4.12 Summary

In this chapter, you have been shown how to do the following:

•   Change the appearance and size of text using the **Font** command or icons.

- Use Paragraph Styles from the **Formatting** bar.
- Align text using the **Paragraph** command or alignment icons.
- Set spacing between lines using the **Paragraph** command.
- Indent a block of text using the **Paragraph** command, the **ruler** and icons.
- Set up bullet points using the **Bullets and Numbering** command or icon.
- Define the Margins and Page Orientation using the **Page Setup** command.
- Create Headers and Footers using the **Headers and Footers** view.
- Add Page Numbers using the **Page Numbers** command.

4.13 Written exercises

4.13.1 Write down simple, step-by-step instructions, assuming you are starting from the main Windows screen, to retrieve a nine page report from floppy disk called **Wordc4d2** and do the following:

(a) Change the six headings in the report to style **Heading1**.

(b) Change line spacing throughout the report to 1.5 spacing.

(c) Add a header containing the author's name and the date and add page numbers at the bottom left of the pages.

4.13.2 Write down simple, step-by-step instructions, assuming you are starting from the main Windows screen, to enable someone to retrieve a document from floppy disk called **Wordc4d1**. This document has been typed but no formatting has been used. Describe how you would enhance the document to look like the one provided in Figure 4.15.

4.14 Practical exercises

4.14.1 Create a new document called **Wordc4d3** on floppy disk to look the same as the letter in Figure 4.15. The margins will differ in your document, so the text may be wrapped differently.

15 The Gables
London
W1 5BN

10th August 1997

Dear Mrs Jenkins,

Subject: Public Library System Proposal

I enclose the updated proposal for the work that will be required to complete the new Public Library Database System. I have included the three changes identified in the meeting of 5th August 1997. These are:

- More than one user may have access the database at one time
- The *Booking Out* screen will include **Author Initials**
- The Title page of the *Outstanding Returns* report will not show the page number.

I would be grateful if you would review the enclosed proposal as soon as possible. Please contact me if you have any queries.

Yours sincerely,

Helen Holding

Figure 4.15 Example letter

4.14.2   Retrieve the curriculum vitae created in the previous chapter, **Wordcv1**, and enhance its appearance as described below. Print it.

(a) Enhance the text using each of the following techniques at least once: bold, underline, italic and font size and change the style of the four sub-headings to be **Heading3**.

(b) Centre justify the main heading and fully justify the Additional Information section. Use 1.5 line spacing throughout and amend qualifications list to use bullet points.

(c) Make sure that it has more than one page (insert a page break if you have to). Add page numbers and a header with your name on it and a footer with the date on the left of the line.

5 │ File Management

5.1 Overview

In this chapter you will learn how to carry out the following techniques:

- List folders and files using My Computer.
- Create, Rename and Delete folders using My Computer.
- Move, Copy and Delete files using My Computer.
- Rename files using My Computer.
- Brief Introduction to Windows Explorer.

5.2 Introduction

Up to now, you will have saved all your Word documents as files directly onto floppy disk, using the floppy disk drive, referred to as the *A: drive*. If you have completed the Word chapters, you should have stored the following files: **Wordbp1, Wordsp1, Wordwp1, Wordwp2, Wordwp3, Wordwp4** and **Wordwp5**. Refer to Figure 5.1.

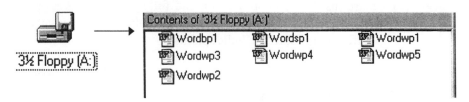

Figure 5.1 Initial file structure

Although there may not be many files currently stored on your disk, you can imagine how complicated it would be to keep track of thirty or forty file names. Even the seven files above can be grouped into two types; Regular Word files, such as **Wordwp1** and **Wordwp2**, and Special Word files, such as **Wordbp1** and **Wordsp1**. It can be very helpful to be able to group files together into directories or *folders*. A folder is created for each group of files and the files are described as being stored *under the folder*. You could create two folders on your disk, called **Regularword** and **Specialword** and place the files *under* the appropriate folder. Refer to Figure 5.2 below:

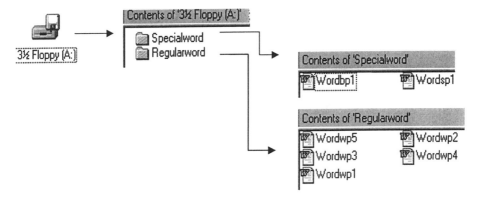

Figure 5.2 File structure 1 on A: drive with two new folders

You may wish to further group your files by creating more folders *under* the existing folders, as in Figure 5.3:

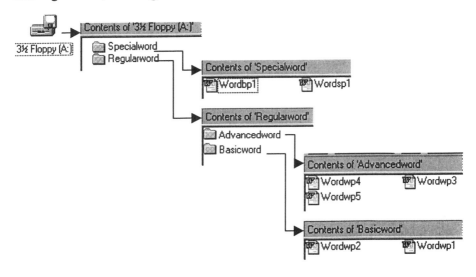

Figure 5.3 File structure 2 on A: drive with two further folders

The folders which make up this file structure should ideally be created before you create and store your files directly under the appropriate folder. What usually happens is that you create a few file stored directly on the disk, as in Figure 5.1. You may then decide to create one or more folders to group your files together. Once you have created the folders, you would then *move* the files *under* the new folders. Word provides tools to enable you to create folders, as well as to move and copy files to different locations within the file structure. You can also delete and rename both files and folders. Word also provides tools to help you view the file structures on your disks. The name to describe all these techniques is *File Management*. There are two main methods of carrying out file management in Windows 95: *My Computer* and *Windows Explorer*. This chapter will explain in detail about My Computer, and will very briefly introduce you to Windows Explorer.

If you have not completed the Word chapters of this book, start Word and create two empty documents, called **Wordsp1** and **Wordbp1**.

5.3   Listing folders and files using My Computer

My Computer is a tool that allows you to see the folders and files currently on your floppy disk or on the hard disk. It displays a series of windows, each containing icons which represent the folders and files at that level of the structure. If you click on a folder icon on any window, the folder will be opened and a window showing the contents of that folder will be displayed.

1.   Double-click the **My Computer** icon on the initial Windows screen. The **My Computer** window will display the different types of input and output devices.

Note that to investigate printing problems, you would open the **Printers** folder icon on the initial **My Computer** window.

2.   Double-click the **(C:)** icon. A window showing the files and folders stored directly under the C: drive is displayed. Refer to Figure 5.4. The contents of your C: drive will differ to those in Figure 5.4.

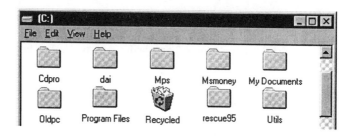

Figure 5.4 C: drive My Computer window

3. One of the folders, **My Documents**, has been set up as the default for storing files. When you save a file, if you forget to change the drive to A:, your file will probably be stored here. Double-click on **My Documents** to see if there are any files stored here. There may be none. Then close the **My Documents** window by clicking the **close** icon on the top right corner of the **My Documents** window.

4. Close the **C:** window currently being shown by clicking the **close** icon on that window. The initial **My Computer** window will become current. You can tell which window is current, since the window and its title bar will be highlighted.

5. Insert your floppy disk and double-click on the **3½ Floppy (A:)** icon. The window will display all the folders and files directly under **A:**. Figure 5.5 shows the files that should be there if you have followed the Word chapters. There may be some additional files you created to carry out the Practical Exercises. Click **View**, then select **Large Icons** if not already selected. You may need to enlarge the **A:** window by clicking and dragging the bottom right corner of the window.

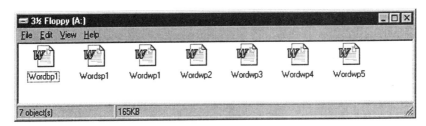

Figure 5.5 Icons shown on A: drive window

5.4 Creating, renaming and deleting folders using My Computer

When you create a new folder, the window you are currently viewing must be the window in which you want your new folder to be placed. Create three new folders as follows:

1. The new folders will be created directly under **A:**, so check that the current window is displaying the contents of the A: drive.

2. Click the **File** command at the top of the **A:** window. Point to **New**, then click **Folder**. An icon representing the new folder will be displayed on the screen. Refer to Figure 5.6. The default name **New**

Folder will be highlighted, expecting you to over-type it with the correct name. In this case, over-type the name of the new folder as **Test-folder**. Press **enter** to activate the change.

3.   Follow the same procedure to create two additional folders in the same place called **Otherword** and **Extraword**.

Now, change the name of the second folder you created as follows:

4.   Click the **Otherword** icon once only to select it, then click the **File** command at the top of the **A:** window. Click **Rename**.

5.   You will be expected to type in the new name of the folder. Type **Specialword**, then press **enter** to activate the change.

Now, delete the third folder you created, **Extraword**. The first thing you must always do before you delete a folder, is to double-click on it to open it and see if there are any files or folders saved under it which you do not wish to delete. If there were, you should double-click on each one to view its contents, and to decide whether to delete the contents or move them to another folder.

6.   Double-click on folder **Extraword** to open it and view what is held under it. In this case an empty window will be displayed. Now that you have checked the contents of **Extraword**, you can safely delete it.

7.   **Close** the **Extraword** window by clicking the **close** icon on the window, then press the **Delete** key or click **File,** then **Delete**. You will be asked if you are sure you wish to delete this folder. Click **Yes**. The **Extraword** folder will be removed from the window.

Q1.   What would happen to any files or folders left in Extraword?

Your basic file structure should look similar to Figure 5.7, although you may have additional files.

Figure 5.6 New Folder icon

Figure 5.7 Existing files and new folders

Note that in **My Computer**, single-clicking on any folder or file will select it for further action. Double-clicking on a folder will open it and display a window with the direct contents of that folder. Double-clicking on a file will automatically open that file with the correct software.

8. Double-click on the file **Wordwp1**. The document **Wordwp1** will be displayed in the Word window. You could start to amend **Wordwp1**, but in this case, just **close** the **Wordwp1** window and the Word window to return to the **My Computer** window.

5.5 Moving, copying and deleting files using My Computer

Now that you have created folder **Specialword**, you can move the two files **Wordsp1** and **Wordbp1** into it. There are two ways to move a file. The first method follows the same four steps as moving text in a document; select the file, cut it to the clipboard, open the folder window where you wish the file to be placed, finally, paste from clipboard. The second method is far simpler, in which you simply click and drag the icon of the file to the folder window where it is to be moved to. Try both methods as follows:

1. Single-click the **Wordsp1** icon to select it, then click the **Edit** command at the top of the window. Click **Cut** to remove the file from its current location. The **Wordsp1** icon will become pale.

2. Double-click the **Specialword** folder icon to open it. An empty window will be displayed. Click the **Edit** command on the **Specialword** window, then click **Paste**. The file will be moved into folder **Specialword** as shown in Figure 5.8.

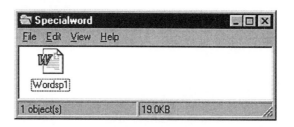

Figure 5.8 File Wordsp1 moved into Specialword folder

3. If the **Specialword** window is covering the **Wordbp1** icon on the **A:** window below, click and drag the blue title bar at the top of the **Specialword** window so that **Wordbp1** can be seen.

4. Click the **Wordbp1** file icon and, keeping the left mouse button depressed, drag the icon such that it is positioned in the **Specialword** window next to **Wordsp1**. Release the mouse button. **Wordbp1** will be moved into the **Specialword** folder.

Q2. Write down the names of the folders and files stored on the A: disk at this point. Show which files are stored in which folder, and which are stored directly on the A: disk, without a folder.

Creating a copy of a file is a similar procedure to moving a file using the menu bar, except that you do not *cut* the file, you *copy* it. You can also use the drag and drop method to copy files, by pressing the **Ctrl** key first. In this case, place a copy of the file **Wordsp1** into folder **Testfolder** as follows:

5. The **Specialword** window should still be current, containing the two files **Wordsp1** and **Wordbp1**. Click **Wordsp1** to select it, then click the **Edit** command on the **Specialword** window and click **Copy**.

6. Double-click the **Testfolder** folder which is where you wish the copied file to be placed. An empty window will be displayed to you, showing you that there is currently nothing in the **Testfolder** folder.

7. Click the **Edit** command on the **Testfolder** window, then click **Paste**. A copy of **Wordsp1** will be placed in the **Testfolder** folder.

8. Hold the **Ctrl** key down on the keyboard and drag and drop the **Wordbp1** file from the **Specialword** window into folder **Testfolder**.

Delete the copy of **Wordsp1** in the **Testfolder** folder as follows:

9. Make sure that the **Testfolder** folder is still the current window. Single-click the **Wordsp1** copy file to select it.

10. Click the **File** command on the **Testfolder** window, then click **Delete**. You will be asked if you are sure you wish to delete the file. Click on **Yes**. The **Wordsp1** copy file will disappear from the **Testfolder** window. Instead of using **File** and **Delete**, you could have pressed the **Delete** key.

The above functions can also be carried out using icons on a toolbar. To view the toolbar, click **View** on the current window, then click **Toolbar**. You may need to enlarge the window to see the whole of the toolbar. Position the mouse pointer on the right edge of the window. Hold the left mouse button down and when a two-headed arrow appears ↔, drag the pointer to the right. Release the button. Refer to the toolbar in Figure 5.10.

| 5.6 | Renaming files using My Computer |

Renaming a file follows the same procedure as renaming a folder. Rename the remaining file in the **Testfolder** folder as follows:

1. Make sure that the **Testfolder** folder is the current window. Single-click the copy of the file **Wordbp1** to select it, then click the **File** command, then **Rename**. Type the new name **Testfile** and press. **enter** to activate the change.

Your **Testfolder** and **Specialword** windows should look similar to Figures 5.9 and 5.10. You may need to reposition the windows using the click and drag technique described preciously to see them simultaneously.
Close all windows on the screen by clicking the **close** icon on each window.

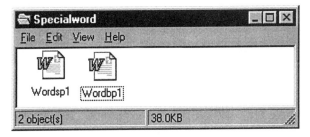

Figure 5.9 Specialword folder

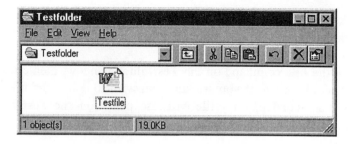

Figure 5.10 Testfolder folder

5.7 Using Windows Explorer

The *Windows Explorer* tool enables you to perform the same functions as My Computer, such as creating folders, moving, renaming and deleting files. However, the method of displaying the file structure is very different. Windows Explorer, similar to the File Manager tool in pre-95 versions of Windows, displays the file structure in a vertical 'family tree'. You can view the contents of each level of the family tree by double-clicking a folder.

Since the functions in Windows Explorer are so similar to those in My Computer, this chapter will only introduce you to this tool very briefly.

1. Click the **Start** icon on the taskbar of the initial Windows screen. Point to **Programs**, then click on **Windows Explorer**. A screen similar to Figure 5.11 will be displayed.

2. If you do not have a toolbar at the top of your Windows Explorer window, click **View**, then click against **Toolbar**.

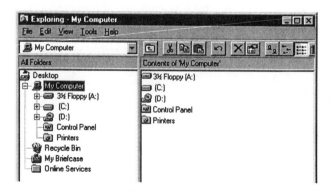

Figure 5.11 Windows Explorer window

3. The **All Folders** section on the left of window displays the vertical file structure, showing only folders, not the files stored under them. If you double-click on a folder, all folders stored directly below it will be shown on the file structure. If you single-click on a folder, its contents, both folders and files, will be displayed on the **Contents** section on the right of the window. Try it out.

As with My Computer, you must select the files or folders first by clicking on them, before you can copy, move, rename or delete them using either the menu bar or the toolbar. A new folder is created using the **File** and **New** menu commands as with My Computer.

4. Click the **close** button on the Windows Explorer window to close Windows Explorer.

5.8   Summary

In this chapter, you will have been shown how to do the following:

- List folders and files by **double-clicking** folder icons in **My Computer**.
- Create new folders using the **File, New** and **Folder** commands in **My Computer**.
- Rename a folder using the **File** and **Rename** commands in **My Computer**.
- Delete folders using the **File** and **Delete** commands in **My Computer**.
- Move and Copy files using the **Edit, Cut, Copy** and **Paste** commands in **My Computer**.
- Delete files using the **File** and **Delete** commands in **My Computer**.
- View and use the toolbar in **My Computer**.
- Rename files using the **File** and **Rename** commands in **My Computer**.
- Use **Windows Explorer** to carry out the same File Management functions as **My Computer**.

5.9   Written exercises

5.9.1   Write down simple, step-by-step instructions, assuming you are starting from the main Windows screen, to enable someone to use My Computer to do the following:

(a) Create a new folder under the **A:** drive called **Weeklytotals**

(b) Rename the folder **Weeklytotals** to new name **Weeklyreps**

(c) Move the files currently residing directly under the **A:** drive called **Wk3sales** and **Wk4sales** into the **Weeklyreps** folder

(d) Rename the **Wk4sales** file in the **Weeklyreps** folder to be called **Wk4purch** and delete the file **Wk3sales**

5.9.2   Write down simple, step-by-step instructions, assuming you are starting from the main Windows screen, to enable someone to use My Computer to do the following tasks, where the current file structure on the floppy disk is shown in Figure 5.12:

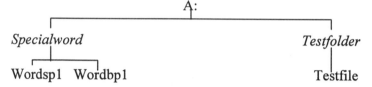

Figure 5.12 Required file structure on A: drive

(a) Create two new folders under **Testfolder** called **Specialcopies** and **Deleteme**.

(b) Rename the folder **Testfolder** to new name **Wordcopies**.

(c) Copy files **Wordsp1** and **Wordbp1** under directory **Special-word** into the new folder **Specialcopies**.

(d) Rename the files **Wordsp1** and **Wordbp1** to new names **Wordsp2** and **Wordbp2** respectively.

(e) Delete the file **Testfile** and the folder **Deleteme**, both from the **Wordcopies** folder.

5.10   Practical exercises

5.10.1   Use **My Computer** to carry out the instructions written down in Question 5.9.2.

5.10.2 Use **My Computer** to create a new folder **Regularword** directly under the **A:** drive and move the five Word documents **Wordwp1, Wordwp2, Wordwp3, Wordwp4** and **Wordwp5** into that new folder. The new file structure should look similar to Figure 5.2

5.10.3 Use **My Computer** to create two further folders under the **Regularword** folder called **Basicword** and **Advancedword** and move the five word files currently under **Regularword** into the two new folders such that the file structure is similar to Figure 5.3.

6 | Microsoft Excel – Getting Started

6.1 Overview

In this chapter you will learn how to carry out the following techniques:

- Start Excel.
- Understand and Use the Excel screen.
- Use the Help feature.
- Move around the Worksheet.
- Enter Text and Numbers into the Worksheet.
- Save and Close a Workbook.
- Create a New Workbook.
- Retrieve a Workbook.
- Preview and Print a Worksheet.
- Exit from Excel and shut down the computer.

6.2 Introduction

Imagine that you wanted to create a Quarterly Report similar to Figure 6.1.

	Jul	Aug	Sep		Total
Expense Report – Third Quarter 1997					
Petrol	£240	£310	£189		£739
Hotel	£120	£185	£ 86		£391
Food & Bar	£ 95	£112	£ 64		£271
Total	£455	£607	£339	£1401	
Expense Budget	£500	£500	£500	£1500	
% Budget Used	*91%*	*121%*	*68%*		*93%*

Figure 6.1 Quarterly Report written using Word

You could use Word to create a very smart looking report. However, if there were thirty-three expense categories instead of three, and one Quarterly Expenses Report for each of the twenty Sales Staff, you can imagine how time consuming it would be to calculate the totals and percentages on each report. Imagine, also, how much time it would take to combine all the reports into an overall quarterly report for the Sales Manager. There is also the risk that the more calculations carried out, the higher the chance of introducing an error.

A spreadsheet package, such as Excel, is designed to help you create exactly this type of document, where there are lists of numbers, with totals and other calculations. The layout of a spreadsheet is similar to a grid, with labelled rows and columns. There are also many pre-set layout styles. See Figure 6.2.

The intersection of each row and column is a called a cell and has its own identification, called an *address*, such as **B3**. You can enter any characters into a cell, from text and numbers, to formulae which can refer to a specific cell address to include in the calculation. The most commonly used formulae are given names and are called *functions*. For example, cell B6 contains a function =SUM(B3:B5), which adds the contents of the cell range B3 to B5. The result is displayed in cell B6.

One of the most useful features of a spreadsheet is that if the value in one of the cells changes, for example the Petrol amount for July is changed to £340, the result displayed in any cells which include the changed cell in their calculations will automatically be recalculated. In this example, the Total in B6 will change to £555 and the % Budget Used in B9 will be 111%.

In Excel, a spreadsheet is called a *Worksheet*. In the above example, each member of staff's individual quarterly expenses would be entered on a separate worksheet. These worksheets would be grouped together in a *Workbook*. When a workbook is saved on the computer, it is saved as a file, in the same way as a *Document* in Word is saved as a file.

	A	B	C	D	E	F
1	Expense Report - Third Quarter 1997					
2		Jul	Aug	Sep	Total	
3	Petrol	£ 240	£ 310	£ 189	£ 739	
4	Hotel	£ 120	£ 185	£ 86	£ 391	
5	Food & Bar	£ 95	£ 112	£ 64	£ 271	
6	Total	£ 455	£ 607	£ 339	£ 1,401	
7						
8	Expense Budget	£ 500	£ 500	£ 500	£ 1,500	
9	% Budget Used	91%	121%	68%	93%	
10						

Figure 6.2 Quarterly Report written using Excel

6.3 Starting Excel and understanding the Excel screen

The following steps explain how to start Excel and describe the main features of the Excel screen:

1. Click the **Start** icon on the main Windows screen. Move the mouse pointer to point to the **Programs** icon. A list of available programs will be displayed.

2. Click on **Microsoft Excel**. The Excel screen with an empty *worksheet* will be displayed as in Figure 6.3. The worksheet is part of a workbook, with the default name of **Book1**. The various parts of the screen are described below:

   The Minimise Buttons, Close Buttons, Menu Bar, Toolbar and Formatting Bar are used in the same way as in Word.

   Editing Line. This line is made up of three elements; **Name Box**, which displays the current cell's address, **Edit Formula** box, which enables you to create and edit a formula in the current cell, and **Formula Bar**, which contains the formula or text contents of the current cell.

   Row and Column Headings. These boxes display the names of the rows and columns in the worksheet. Clicking on them will select whole rows or columns.

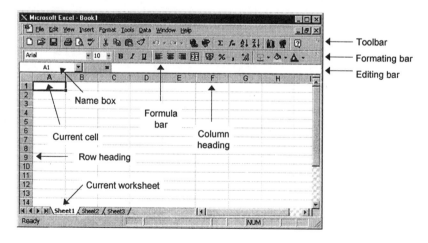

Figure 6.3 Basic Excel screen

Current Cell. The address of this cell is displayed in the **Name Box** and the contents of the cell, either text or formula, are displayed in the **Formula Bar**. If the cell contains a formula, the result will be displayed in the current cell on the worksheet.

Current Worksheet. The workbook will display many worksheets, layered one above the other. The current worksheet will always be shown on the top and highlighted.

Scroll Bars. Dragging the grey box or clicking the scroll arrows allows you to control which area of your worksheet is in view.

Q1.   *What is the initial empty worksheet called and what is the address of the current cell?*

6.4   Using help

The Help facility used in Excel is the same as that used in Word, with the exception that the main help tool is called *Microsoft Excel Help* instead of *Microsoft Word Help*. Refer to Chapter 2 for further information about Help.

Version 7   The main help tools are **Microsoft Excel Help Topics** and **Answer Wizard**.

6.5   Moving around the worksheet

There are several methods of moving around a worksheet to select a new *current cell*, through which text, numbers, formulae and functions are entered.

1.   Move the mouse such that its pointer is on cell **E10**, then **click** the left mouse button. Cell **E10** will be outlined and "E10" will appear in the **Name Box**. Since **E10** is empty, the Formula Bar will be empty.

To view a different part of your worksheet on the screen, use the scroll bar as described below. You can then use your mouse to select the current cell.

2.   Click the lower, paler section of the vertical scroll bar. The next screen-full of cells will be shown. Click on cell **G24** to make that cell current.

3. Click the **scroll arrows** on the vertical and horizontal scroll bars to move the cells on the screen up or down, or left and right accordingly.

Another way to move around is to use the **arrow**, **Home** and **Ctrl** keys.

4. Press each of the four arrow keys ↑ , ←, ↓ and → to move the current cell to the cell above, left, below and right respectively.

5. Press the **Home** key to move the current cell to the start of the row, then keep the **Ctrl** key depressed while you press the **Home** key to move the current cell to cell **A1**.

Note that when you press any key in conjunction with the **Ctrl** key, press the **Ctrl** key first, then whilst keeping it depressed, press the other key.

Q2. What do the following two combinations of key depressions do?
*(a) → and **Ctrl** together (b) ↓ and **Ctrl** together*

6.6 Entering text and numbers

Entering text into a worksheet is done by entering text into each cell in turn. You must first make the cell current, then type in the text.

1. Make cell **B3** current. Type the text **Sarah.** Press **Enter.** The word **Sarah** will be left justified. This is the *default* justification for text.

2. Make cell **B4** current. Type the number **850** and press **Enter.** The number will be right justified. This is the default for numbers.

3. Use the same method to complete the worksheet in Figure 6.4.

	A	B	C	D	E	F
1						
2						
3		Sarah	Tony	David	Rachel	
4		850	1500	650	1000	
5						
6						
7		350	605	300	75	
8		200	210	40	620	
9		97	15	175	140	
10		115	20	230	135	

Figure 6.4 Worksheet with text and numbers

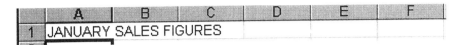

Figure 6.5 Worksheet with title in cell A1

4.   Make the cell **A1** the current cell and type in **JANUARY SALES FIGURES**. Press **enter**. Refer to Figure 6.5.

Q3.   *What do you think the contents of cell B1 are?*

5.   Make cell **B1** current. The **Formula Bar** will be empty because there is no text in **B1**. The text was entered in cell **A1**. Since cells **B1** and **C1** are empty, there is room to display **A1** over these empty cells.

6.   Make cell **A1** the current cell and look at the **Formula Bar**. You will see the whole text **JANUARY SALES FIGURES** displayed there.

7.   Make cell **A4** current and type the text **Projected Sales**. Press **Enter**. Since cell **B4** is not empty, the text from cell **A4** cannot spill over it, and is therefore not shown on the screen. It is shown in the **Formula Bar** when you make cell **A4** current.

8.   Complete the **A** column in your worksheet to look like Figure 6.6.

	A	B	C	D	E	F
1	JANUARY	SALES FIGURES				
2						
3		Sarah	Tony	David	Rachel	
4	Projected	850	1500	650	1000	
5						
6	Actual Sales:					
7	Speakers	350	605	300	75	
8	Headsets	200	210	40	620	
9	Sockets	97	15	175	140	
10	Cables	115	20	230	135	
11	Total Sales					
12	5% Commission					
13	Net Sales					
14						
15	% Sales Achieved					
16						
17	Next Months Sales					

Figure 6.6 Worksheet with Column A completed

6.7 Saving and closing a workbook

Saving a workbook in Excel is similar to saving a document in Word. Refer to Chapter 2 for further details about saving files.

1.   Insert your floppy disk into the base unit and click **File**, then **Save**.

2.   Click the **down arrow** next to the **Save in** box. The box lists all possible locations you can save your files to. Click **3½ Floppy (A:)**.

3.   The name displayed in the **File name** box is a *default* workbook name, **Book1**. Position the cursor at the end of the default file name and use the **backspace** key to delete it. Type **Saleswb1** instead.

4.   Click the **Save** box and watch the *egg timer* icon appear whilst the file is being saved. Your workbook will be saved as a file on the floppy disk called **Saleswb1.xls**. All Excel files have the **.xls** suffix, although in Windows, you are not usually shown the suffix.

Note that instead of clicking on **File** and then **Save** to get the save window, you could have just clicked the **Save** icon on the toolbar.

5.   Click the **Workbook Close** icon on the top right of the worksheet. Do not click the **Excel Close** icon above it. Stay in Excel.

Q4.   If you changed the workbook before closing it, what would happen?

6.8 Creating a new workbook

When you first start Excel, a new workbook is automatically created, called **Book1**. Once you have saved the first workbook or opened another file, if you create a new workbook, it will be given the next default name, **Book2**.

1.   Click **File**, then **New**. The **New** window will be displayed. Click **OK**. A new workbook **Book2** will be displayed. The workbook name, **Book2**, will appear on the title bar at the top of the window.

2.   In this case, you do not need the new workbook, so close it by clicking the **Workbook Close** icon. The workbook underneath **Book2** will be displayed, **Saleswb1**.

Q5.   Were you asked if you wanted to save the workbook? Why?

Instead of clicking **File**, then **New**, you could have just clicked on the **New** icon in the toolbar.

6.9   Retrieving a workbook

When you retrieve a workbook from disk, it goes into temporary store in the computer. It can then be changed and saved, or just be read or copied before closing it without saving. Refer to Chapter 2 for details on retrieving a file.

1.   Click **File**, then **Open**. The Open window will be displayed. Insert your floppy disk.

Instead of clicking **File**, then **Open**, you could have just clicked on the **Open** icon in the toolbar.

2.   Click the **down scroll arrow** next to the **Look in** box and select **3½ Floppy (A:)**. The Excel files on the floppy disk will be listed. Click **Saleswb1,** then click **Open. Saleswb1** will appear on your screen.

6.10   Previewing a worksheet

Excel allows you to view a miniature version of your worksheets so that you can see what they will look like when printed.

1.   Click **File** on the menu bar, then click **Print Preview**. A miniature version of **Saleswb1** will be displayed. Refer to Figure 6.7.

2.   Click the **Zoom** box to zoom in on a section of the worksheet, then click **Zoom** again to return to the miniature view. Click the box with the word **Close** to get back to the previous screen.

Instead of clicking **File,** then **Print Preview**, you could just have clicked the **Print Preview** icon on the toolbar.

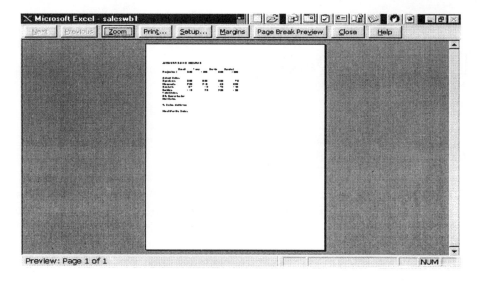

Figure 6.7 Print Preview

6.11 Printing a worksheet

To print a worksheet in Excel you either click the print icon, which will print one copy of the default range of your current worksheet or you can use the Print command which allows you to request various printing options. The default range in a worksheet is from cell **A1** to the bottom right cell that has had an entry typed into it. You may wish to refer to Chapter 3 for further information about printing and print queues.

1.   Print one copy of sheet 1 of your **Saleswb1** workbook by clicking the **Print** icon 🖨 on the toolbar.

This time you are going to request two copies of your worksheet as follows:

2.   Click the **File** command on the menu bar, then click **Print**. The screen shown in Figure 6.8 will be displayed. Your printer details may differ. Refer to Figure 6.8.

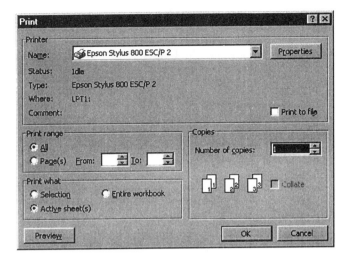

Figure 6.8 Print window

There are four main sections in the Print window:

- **Printer** provides details about the printer you are using.
- **Page range** allows you to select whether you wish to print all the pages in the worksheets or a specific range of pages, such as 4 or 1, 2, 3 or 1–6.
- **Print what** allows you to select which worksheets in the workbook you wish to print. The selected worksheets will be printed with the same range as specified in the **Page range** section. The default is **Active sheets**.
- **Copies** will allow you enter how many copies of the print you require.

3.   Click on the **up arrow** in the **Number of copies** box to get the number **2** to appear in the box, then click on the **OK** box.

6.12 Exiting from Excel and shutting down the computer

You should always remember to close all workbooks before exiting Excel.

1.   Close the current workbook **Saleswb1** by clicking the **Workbook Close** icon on the top right of the worksheet.

2.   Click **File**, then **Exit**. Excel will close, taking you back to the Windows main screen. Alternatively, you could have clicked the **Application Close** icon ☒ in the top right corner of the screen.

3. Remove your floppy disk. Click the **Start** icon then click the **Shut Down** command. The computer screen will ask if you are sure you want to shut down the computer. Click on **Yes**. A screen message will let you know when you can safely turn off your computer on the base unit unless it turns itself off automatically.

6.13 Summary

In this chapter, you will have been shown how to do the following:

- Start Excel using the **Start** icon and the **Programs** and **Excel** commands.
- Recognise and use features of the Excel screen.
- Use **Microsoft Excel Help** to find the Help screen for a particular task.
- Move around a worksheet using the mouse, scroll buttons and arrows keys.
- Enter Text and Numbers into the Worksheet.
- Save a Workbook using the **File** and **Save** commands or **Save** icon.
- Close a Workbook using the **Workbook Close** icon.
- Create a new Workbook using the **File** and **New** commands or **New** icon.
- Retrieve a Workbook using the **File** and **Open** commands or **Open** icon.
- Preview a Worksheet using the **File** and **Print Preview** commands or **Preview** icon.
- Print a worksheet using the **File** and **Print** commands or the **Print** icon.
- Exit from Excel using the **Close** icon and the **Exit** commands.
- Shut down the computer using the **Start** and **Shut Down** commands.

6.14 Written exercises

6.14.1 Write down simple, step-by-step instructions, assuming you are starting from the main Windows screen, to enable someone to start Excel and do the following:

(a) Start **Excel** and type **Name** in cell **A1**. Move to the cell **D1** and type **Address**. Move to cell **A2** and type your name then move to cell **D2** and type the first line of your address. Enter two further names and addresses in **A3** and **D3**, **A4** and **D4**. Save then close the workbook on floppy disk as **Addresswb1.**

(b) Retrieve **Addresswb1** from you floppy disk, preview it, then print just the one default copy of it. Close the workbook.

6.14.2   Write down simple, step-by-step instructions, assuming you are starting from the main Windows screen, to enable someone to create a new Workbook called **Finanrep1**, stored in floppy disk as follows:

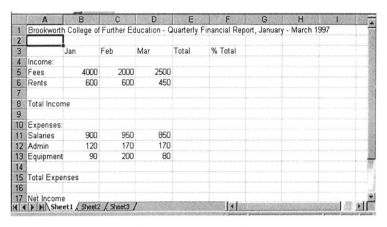

Figure 6.9 Finanrep1

6.15 Practical exercises

6.15.1   Use **Excel** to create a wordbook called **Finanrep1** on floppy disk by following the instructions provided in exercise 6.14.2. Preview it then print out a copy.

6.15.2   Create a personal budget similar to Finanrep1, reflecting your own personal income and expenses, using more rows and columns if necessary. Leave space for the **Total Income**, **Total Expenses** and **Net Income** calculations to be added in later practical exercises. Save the workbook as **Persbudg1**. Preview it then print out one copy.

6.15.3   Create a new workbook on floppy disk called **Monthtest1**. Use **Microsoft Excel Help** to find the help screen to tell you how to automatically fill a series of cells with incremental values, such as 1,2,3,4.... Type **Jan** and **Feb** in cells **A1** and **B1** respectively, then use the help instructions to fill cells **C1** to **L1** with **Mar** to **Dec**.

7 Microsoft Excel – Cell Manipulation and Worksheet Layout

7.1 Overview

In this chapter you will learn how to carry out the following techniques:

- Copy your workbook.
- Edit the contents of a cell.
- Select a range of cells.
- Sort a range of cells.
- Copy, move and clear cell contents.
- Insert and delete rows and columns.
- Align and format text.
- Change column and row width.
- Use Autoformat to enhance the worksheet.
- Define the page layout.

7.2 Introduction

In the previous chapter you were shown how to enter text and numbers into a worksheet, how to save, retrieve and print a workbook and how to move around the worksheet.

This chapter goes further in explaining how to improve the look and layout of your worksheet and how to manipulate the contents of the cells. You will be shown how to select, sort, move, copy and clear a range of cells, and how to insert and change the width of rows and columns. You will also be shown how to align and format your text, as well as how to apply standard style lay-out to your worksheet.

In the previous chapter you will have created a simple workbook **Saleswb1**. You will need to use that workbook as the basis or this chapter, but instead of changing **Saleswb1**, you will take a copy of it first under a new name, and then proceed to work from the copy. This will leave the original version unchanged. This is a useful method of retaining several versions of workbook.

7.3 Copying a Workbook

When you retrieve a workbook, change it and then save it again, the changed version will overwrite the previous version saved on disk. To keep the previous version, you must copy your original workbook under a new name and then edit the new version. Since you are going to alter the contents of the **Saleswb1** workbook, take a copy of it using the *Save As* command as follows:

1.   Start **Excel** then insert your floppy disk into the disk drive and retrieve the workbook **Saleswb1** from your floppy disk.

2.   Click **File**, then click **Save As...** The same screen will be displayed as when you first save a workbook. Refer to Chapter 6.

3.   Change the file name from **Saleswb1** to **Saleswb2** and click the **Save** box. There are now two identical copies of this document on disk, **Saleswb1** and **Saleswb2**. **Saleswb2** is the workbook currently displayed on the screen.

7.4 Editing the contents of a cell

When you enter any characters into a cell by typing the text and then pressing **enter** or an **arrow** key, the new text will overwrite any existing text. To amend the contents of a cell without overwriting, you must use the **Editing Bar**.

1.   Make cell **C3** current, then click the **Formula bar** in the **Editing Bar**. Change **Tony** to **Tom** in the **Formula bar**, then click the **tick** shown in the **Edit Formula** box. Refer to Figure 7.1.

Version 7   The **Function Wizard** icon is included in the **Editing Bar** instead of the equals sign, =.

2.   Make cell **D3** current, click the **Formula bar** and change **David** to **Katie**. This time, click the **cross** and the change will not be copied to the worksheet.

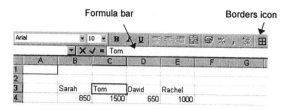

Figure 7.1 Editing bar and Borders icon

7.5 Selecting a range of cells

In the same way that in Word you can select a block of text to format, copy, move or delete, you can select a block or *range* of cells in Excel.

1. Make cell **A3** current, then, whilst keeping the left mouse button depressed, drag the mouse to the right until cells **A3**, **B3**, **C3**, **D3** and **E3** are all highlighted. Release the mouse button. These cells can also be referred to as the range **A3** to **E3**, or **A3:E3**. Refer to Figure 7.2.

	A	B	C	D	E	F
1	JANUARY SALES FIGURES					
2						
3		Sarah	Tom	David	Rachel	
4	Projected	850	1500	650	1000	
5						

Figure 7.2 Selected range of cells A3:E3

2. Apply an underlining border to the cells by clicking the **down arrow** to the right of the **Borders** icon ⊞ on the Formatting bar. The Borders icon will show the most recent type of border selected, so the borders icon on your toolbar may differ. A window showing the types of border available will be displayed. Click the border with just a line at the bottom, ⊞. Refer to Figure 7.3.

Q1 *What range of cells should be selected if you were to apply an underline border to the* ***Cables*** *row of figures?*

	A	B	C	D	E
3		Sarah	Tom	David	Rachel
4	Projected	850	1500	650	1000
5					

Figure 7.3 Underline border applied to range A3:E3

3.   Carry out the same procedure to apply an underlining border to the **Ca-bles** row of figures, but this time, you do not need to click the **down arrow** on the **Borders** icon. Since the underline border was the most recent border used, it is displayed as the default border icon. Simply click the **Borders** icon.

4.   Select the range **A3:E11** by clicking on cell **A3**, then, whilst holding down the left mouse button, drag the pointer to cell **E11**. This will highlight the required range of cells. Apply a four-sided border by clicking the **down arrow** next to the borders icon and select the border icon with four sides outlined ⊞.

5.   Remove the borders by selecting range **A3:E11** again, then apply the border selection which has no border around it at all. Then re-apply the border underline to cells **A3:E3**. Click the **Save** icon to save the workbook **Saleswb2**.

7.6   Sort a range of cells

The **Data** option in the menu bar offers many tools to enable you to manipulate the data in your worksheet. The **Sort** tool, which enables you to sort a range of cells into a specific order is explained briefly below. The other Data features are not covered in this book.

1.   Select cell range **A7:E10**, then click **Data** on the menu bar. Click **Sort**. The following window will appear. Refer to Figure 7.4.

Figure 7.4 Sort data window

Cell manipulation and worksheet layout   77

2.   You are going to sort the range of cells in column A into ascending order, so simply click **OK**. Refer to Figure 7.5.

7	Cables	115	20	230	135
8	Headsets	200	210	40	620
9	Sockets	97	15	175	140
10	Speakers	350	605	300	75

Figure 7.5 Sorted cells

3.   Click the **Undo** icon ✏ on the tool bar to remove the sort.

Instead of using the **Data** and **Sort** menu commands to carry out this simple sort, you could have clicked the sort Ascending icon $\frac{A}{Z}\downarrow$.

7.7   Copying cell contents

Copying cell contents in Excel is similar to copying blocks of text in Word. First, select the cell or range of cells to be copied then copy the range of cells to a place in the computer's memory, called the *clipboard.* You must next decide where you wish the copy of the cells to be placed and then *paste* the copy of the cells from the clipboard to the selected range of cells. If you select one cell only, the copied cells will be placed such that the top left cell is placed over the selected cell.

1.   Select range **A7:A10**. Click the **Edit** command, then click **Copy**. The selected range has a flashing border to show that it is in the clipboard.

2.   Make cell **D9** current, then click the **Edit** command, then **Paste**. All four cells should have been copied, the top cell overwriting cell **D9**. Refer to Figure 7.6.

6	Actual Sales:				
7	Speakers	350	605	300	75
8	Headsets	200	210	40	620
9	Sockets	97	15	Speakers	140
10	Cables	115	20	Headsets	135
11	Total Sales			Sockets	
12	5% Commission			Cables	
13	Net Sales				

Figure 7.6 Copying cells A7:A10 to cells D9:D12

3.   Make any cell on the worksheet current and the highlighting will disappear. Press the **Esc** key.

Q2. *What happens to the flashing border when the Esc key is pressed?*

4.   Select range **B3:C3** and click the **Copy** icon ▣ on the toolbar. Select range **A13:B13** and click the **Paste** icon ▣ on the toolbar. Make any cell current and press the **Esc** key to remove the flashing border and highlighting as before. Refer to Figure 7.7.

		Sarah	Tom	David	Rachel
3		Sarah	Tom	David	Rachel
4	Projected	850	1500	650	1000
5					
6	Actual Sales:				
7	Speakers	350	605	300	75
8	Headsets	200	210	40	620
9	Sockets	97	15	Speakers	140
10	Cables	115	20	Headsets	135
11	Total Sales			Sockets	
12	5% Commission			Cables	
13	Sarah	Tom			

Figure 7.7 Copying cells B3:C3 to cells A13:B13

Another quick way to copy cells is using the *drag and drop* method, whereby you select the range of cells to be copied, then hold the **Ctrl** key down whilst you drag the copy of the selected cells to the appropriate position on the worksheet.

7.8   Moving cell contents

Moving cell contents is similar to copying cell contents, except that instead of copying the selected range of cells the clipboard, they are removed or *cut* from the worksheet and placed in the clipboard.

1.   Select range **A7:E7** and click the **Edit** command, then click **Cut**. The selected range has a flashing border to show that it is in the clipboard.

2.   Select cell **A14** and click the **Paste** icon. The contents of cells **A7:E7** have been placed in cells **A14:E14** and the flashing border around **A7:E7** has gone, since the cells are no longer in the clipboard. Make any cell current to remove the highlighting. Refer to Figure 7.8.

7					
8	Headsets	200	210	40	620
9	Sockets	97	15	Speakers	140
10	Cables	115	20	Headsets	135
11	Total Sales			Sockets	
12	5% Commission			Cables	
13	Sarah	Tom			
14	Speakers	350	605	300	75

Figure 7.8 Moving cells A7:E7 to cells A14:E14

Instead of clicking the **Edit** and **Cut** commands, you could click the **Cut** icon ✄ on the toolbar.

Another quick way to move cells is to use the same *drop and drag* method as described to copy cells, but without holding down the **Ctrl** key.

7.9   Clearing cell contents

There are three main ways to clear the contents of a cell: the space bar, the **Edit** and **Clear** commands and the **Delete** key.

1.   Clear **B8** by making cell **B8** current then press the **space bar.** Select range **B3:C3.** Click the **Edit** command, then point to **Clear.** Click **All.** Cells **B3** and **C3** should be empty with no underlining.

The **All** type of **Clear** command will clear both the contents and formatting in a cell. **Formats** and **Contents** will clear just the formatting or just the contents. Pressing the **Delete** key will also clear the contents of selected cells and leave the formatting.

2.   Make cell **D3** current, then as above, use the **Edit** and **Clear** commands, but this time click **Formats.** Make cell **E3** current and use the **Edit, Clear** and **Contents** commands. Your screen should look like Figure 7.9.

	A	B	C	D	E	F
1	JANUARY SALES FIGURES					
2						
3				David		
4	Projected	850	1500	650	1000	

Figure 7.9 Cleared cells

3.   Save workbook **Saleswb2,** then **close** the workbook. Stay in Excel.

7.10 Inserting and deleting rows and columns

One of the useful features of Excel is the ability to insert rows and columns without affecting the rest of the worksheet. Insert a row of figures for fuses and a new member of sales staff, Emily:

1. Click the **Open** icon on the toolbar and retrieve workbook **Saleswb1** from your floppy disk. Click **File**, then click **Save As** and rename the workbook **Saleswb3**. Click **Save**.

2. Make cell **A10** current. Click the **Insert** command, then click **Rows**. A new row 10 will be inserted above the current cell.

3. Click the box at the top of column D with the letter **D** in it. Column **D** will be highlighted. Click the **Insert** command, then click **Columns**. A new column will be inserted to the left of the highlighted column.

4. Complete the contents of row **10** and column **D**. Refer to Figure 7.10.

	A	B	C	D	E	F
1	JANUARY SALES FIGURES					
2						
3		Sarah	Tony	Emily	David	Rachel
4	Projected :	850	1500	920	650	1000
5						
6	Actual Sales:					
7	Speakers	350	605	560	300	75
8	Headsets	200	210	120	40	620
9	Sockets	97	15	25	175	140
10	Fuses	45	25	125	160	75
11	Cables	115	20	210	230	135

Figure 7.10 Completed row 10 and column D

5. Delete row 5 as follows: Click the **5** box at the left of row **5**. The whole row will be highlighted. Click the **Edit** command, then click **Delete**. The old row 5 will disappear, and all rows below will be moved up. Save the workbook **Saleswb3**.

7.11 Aligning and formatting text

There are two methods of aligning text; aligning text within its own cell, and aligning the contents of one cell only across a selected range of cells.

1. Select cell range **B3:F3**. Click the **Centre** alignment icon ☰. Refer to Figure 7.12. The text in each cell will be centred in its cell.

2.   Select cell range **A1:F1**. Click the **Merge and Centre icon** 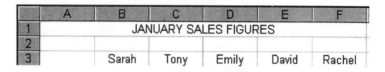. Refer to Figure 7.12 below. The text in cell **A1** will be centred across the selected range. Refer to Figure 7.11.

	A	B	C	D	E	F
1			JANUARY SALES FIGURES			
2						
3		Sarah	Tony	Emily	David	Rachel

Figure 7.11 Cell and range alignments

There are several other alignment possibilities in **Excel** including vertical alignment and wrapping the text within the cell if necessary. These functions can all be carried out using the **Format, Cells** and **Alignment** commands.

Text in a worksheet can be formatted in the same way as in Word, with some additional formats, such as currency and percentages. Refer to Figure 7.12.

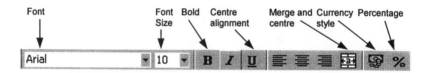

Figure 7.12 Formatting bar

3.   Select cell **A1**. Change the font size to 18 by clicking the **down scroll arrow** at the right of the font size box on the formatting bar. Click **18**. Then click the **Bold** icon **B**.

4.   Prefix the numbers with a £ sign, by first selecting the range **B4:F10**, then clicking the **Currency Style** icon. Refer to Figure 7.13.

Your worksheet may display dollars instead of pounds, depending on how your computer has been set up. If the columns in your worksheet are too narrow for the currency style on some cells, the cells will display a row of # signs. You will be shown how to widen your columns in the next section.

The **Format, Cells** and **Number** commands allow you to select other currency and number-based styles if those offered on the toolbar are not sufficient.

	A	B	C	D	E	F
1	JANUARY SALES FIGURES					
2						
3		Sarah	Tony	Emily	David	Rachel
4	Projected :	£ 850.00	£ 1,500.00	£ 920.00	£ 650.00	£ 1,000.00
5	Actual Sales:					
6	Speakers	£ 350.00	£ 605.00	£ 560.00	£ 300.00	£ 75.00
7	Headsets	£ 200.00	£ 210.00	£ 120.00	£ 40.00	£ 620.00
8	Sockets	£ 97.00	£ 15.00	£ 25.00	£ 175.00	£ 140.00
9	Fuses	£ 45.00	£ 25.00	£ 125.00	£ 160.00	£ 75.00
10	Cables	£ 115.00	£ 20.00	£ 210.00	£ 230.00	£ 135.00

Figure 7.13 Formatted heading and currency prefixes

7.12 Changing column and row widths

It is often the case that a row heading or a number in a cell is too wide for the column and you therefore need to increase the width of the column. The two most useful methods to change column width are to click and drag the side of the column, or to allow Excel to fit the size of the column to the text within it.

1. Widen column **A** such that the text in cell **A4, Projected Sales,** can be seen. Position the mouse pointer on the right side of the **A** box at the top of column **A**. Press the mouse button and holding it down, drag the mouse to the right until the column is wide enough to see all the text in cell **A4.** Release the mouse button. Notice that a yellow box appears above the worksheet displaying the column width.

Version 7 The column width is shown in the **Name Box** on the **Editing Bar** while you widen a column.

Q3. What is the final width of the column?

2. Change the text in cell **A17** to **Next Months Projected Sales** and select column **A** by clicking the **A** box at the top of the column.

3. Allow Excel to fit the column to the text by clicking the **Format** commands, then point to **Column** and click **AutoFit Selection.** The column width will be enlarged.

Q4. What is the column width? [Hint: Click the right side of the A box]

4. Increase the width of any columns which currently contain # signs.

Cell manipulation and worksheet layout 83

Row widths can be amended in the same way, by clicking and dragging the bottom side of the row heading boxes or using the **Format** and **Row** commands.

7.13 Using autoformat to enhance the worksheet

Although it is possible to apply borders and formatting to the cells in the worksheet yourself, Excel has a tool which applies a selected style setting to your worksheet. This includes text formatting, underlining and shading, thereby enabling you to produce professional and consistent looking worksheets very quickly.

1.   Enter the text **Totals** in cell **G3**. Then select cell range **A3:G11**.

2.   Click the **Format** then the **Autoformat** commands. The following window will be displayed:

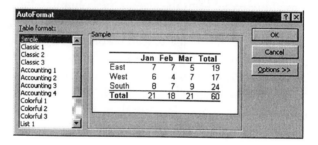

Figure 7.14 Autoformat window

3.   Click each of the entries in the **Table Format** list to see their styles displayed in the **Sample** box. Finally, click on **Simple**, then click **OK**. Refer to Figure 7.15.

	Sarah	Tony	Emily	David	Rachel	Total
Projected Sales	£850.00	£1,500.00	£920.00	£650.00	£1,000.00	
Actual Sales						
Speakers	£350.00	£ 605.00	£560.00	£300.00	£ 75.00	
Headgate	£200.00	£ 210.00	£120.00	£ 40.00	£ 620.00	
Sockets	£ 97.00	£ 15.00	£ 25.00	£175.00	£ 140.00	
Fuses	£ 45.00	£ 25.00	£125.00	£160.00	£ 75.00	
Cables	£115.00	£ 20.00	£210.00	£230.00	£ 135.00	
Total Sales						
5% Commision						

Figure 7.15 Autoformat Simple

4.   Save the worksheet **Saleswb3** by clicking the **Save** icon.

7.14 Defining the page layout

It is very useful when using a worksheet to be able to specify which way up the paper should be used, either portrait or landscape. It is also very useful to be able to specify whether you wish to see gridlines on your printed worksheet or not. These and other settings can all be applied using the **Page Setup** command.

1.   Click on the **File**, then the **Page Setup** commands. The **Page** window will be displayed in front of other windows. If it is not at the front, click the **Page** tab. Refer to Figure 7.16.

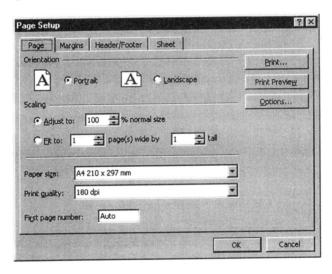

Figure 7.16 Page Setup, Page window

2.   Click the white circle next to **Landscape**, under the **Orientation** heading. Click the **Print Preview** box. Notice how the picture of a page is now on its side, landscape.

3.   Click the **Setup** box at the top of the preview screen and change from **Landscape** to **Portrait** again. The **Setup** dialogue box is now in front of the preview screen. Click **OK** to preview.

4.   Click **Setup** again. Click the **Sheet** tab then click the white box next to **Gridlines** under the **Print** heading to put a tick there. Click **OK**.

Q5. *What is different about the preview of your worksheet this time ?*

5.   Click **Setup** again and change back to no gridlines by clicking the tick next to **Gridlines** to get rid of it. Click **OK** again to see the difference, then click **Close**.

6.   Save the workbook **Saleswb3**, then **close** the workbook and **close** Excel. Remove your floppy disk, then **Shut Down** the computer as described in the previous chapter.

7.15 Summary

In this chapter, you will have been shown how to do the following:

*   Copy your workbook using **File** and **Save As** commands.
*   Edit the contents of a cell using the **Editing Bar** and **Formula bar**.
*   Select a range of cells using the mouse.
*   Sort a range of cells using the **Data** and **Sort** commands and **Sort** icon.
*   Copy, move and clear cell contents using the **Edit, Copy, Cut, Paste** and **Clear** commands as well as the **Copy, Cut** and **Paste** icons.
*   Insert and delete rows and columns using the **Insert, Rows** and **Columns** commands and the **Edit** and **Delete** commands.
*   Align and format text using the **Align** and **Currency** icons.
*   Change column and row width using the mouse to click and drag and the **Format, Column** and **Autofit** commands.
*   Enhance the worksheet using the **Format** and **Autoformat** commands.
*   Define the page layout using the **Page Setup, Page** and **Sheet** commands.

7.16 Written exercises

7.16.1 Write down simple, step-by-step instructions, assuming you are starting from the main Windows screen, to enable someone to use **Excel** to retrieve a workbook **Monthlyrep1** from floppy disk.

	A	B	C	D	E	F
1	Monthly Report - April 1997					
2						
3		Assign1	Assign2	Exam1	Exam2	Overall
4	J. Cox	12	15	14	21	
5	B. Barolo	87	89	75	72	
6	G. Yung	56	64	71	62	
7	K. Smith	52	13	45	43	
8	D. Tanaka	62	59	63	68	

Figure 7.17 Monthlyrep1

Save it on the floppy disk under a new name **Monthlyrep2** and change it as follows:

(a) Insert a column between Assign2 and Exam1 called **Total Assign** and insert a column between Exam2 and Overall called **Total Exam**.

(b) Use the click and drag method to widen the two new columns to fit the text and use **Autoformat** to apply the **Classic3** style to the worksheet table.

(c) Use **Page Setup** to change the orientation ot tne page to landscape. **Print Preview** and **Print** one copy of it.

7.16.2 Write down simple, step-by-step instructions, assuming you are starting from the main Windows screen, to enable someone to use **Excel** to retrieve a workbook **Finanrep1** from floppy disk and copy it on the floppy disk under the name **Finanrep2**. Refer to the exercise in 6.14.2 in the previous chapter. Carry out the following changes to **Finanrep2**:

(a) Change the title to **Brookworth University – Financial Report – First Quarter 1997** and set to bold and size 14.

(b) Select cell range **A3:F3** and add an underline border. Select cell range **A1:H1** and centre the title text in that range.

(c) Insert a row between **Fees** and **Rents** called **Consultancy** and copy cell range **B12:D12** into new empty cells **B6:D6**. Widen column **A** using **Autofit Selection**.

7.17.1   Use **Excel** to retrieve a workbook called **Finanrep1** from floppy disk, created in the previous chapter, copy it and change the copy following the instructions provided in part two of the previous section.

7.17.2   Retrieve the personal budget **Persbudg1** from your floppy disk created in the Chapter 2 and copy the worksheet onto floppy disk under name **Persbudg2**. Insert a row to show a new expenses category in your budget and apply the **Currency** format to the numbers on your worksheet. Move the title of your worksheet one cell to the right. **Save Persbudg2**, then **Save As** to floppy disk under the file name **Persbudg3**.

Retrieve **Persbudg2** and apply an **Autoformat** style to your worksheet. Save again and print off one copy. Retrieve **Persbudg3** and **Centre** justify the column headings and **Merge and Centre** the main worksheet heading across the top of your worksheet. Save again and print off one copy.

7.17.3   Create a new workbook on floppy disk called **Chapt7prac3** and use **Microsoft Excel Help** to find the help screen to tell you how to align your text vertically in the cell and how to wrap the text in a cell. Try to create the following worksheet

Computer Science Essay Checklist	Draft Written	Draft Reviewed	1st Edition Written	1st Edition Reviewed	Completed
What are the advantages and limitations of the six main types of Power Tool					
What is an Expert System					
Virtual Reality - the way forward or the way out					

Figure 7.18 Chapt7prac3

8 Microsoft Excel – Functions and Formulae

8.1 Overview

In this chapter you will learn how to carry out the following techniques:

- Fill a range by example.
- Use formulae.
- Use functions.
- Use absolute cell addresses.
- Freeze panes on the screen.

8.2 Introduction

In the previous two chapters you were shown how to create and copy a simple worksheet, how to move and copy cells and how to enhance its appearance and layout.

One of the major features of a worksheet, is the ability to carry out mathematical calculations, called *Formulae,* referring to the addresses of cells rather than to their contents. For example, cell **C6** may contain the calculation **=C4+C5**. The result of the calculation, adding together the contents of cells **C4** and **C5**, is displayed in cell **C6** on the worksheet. If the contents of cell **C4** were amended, the resulting total in cell **C6** would automatically be updated and displayed on the worksheet. Some formulae are used frequently, and have been given names to make using them simpler and faster. These formulae are called *Functions*. The function **SUM** calculates the total of a range of cells.

If the formula in cell **C6** were to be copied to cell **D6**, Excel would record by how many rows or columns the new cell address **D6** differs from the old cell address **C6**. Excel would then automatically change any addresses in the function or formula in cell **D6** by the same number of row or columns. In this example, the addresses in the formula would all be increased by one column to **=D4+D5**. In some cases, you do not want a cell address to be changed in

89

this way. By inserting a dollar sign before each part of the cell address, Excel will recognise that this address must not be changed. This type of cell address is called an *Absolute* cell address.

You will also be shown how to affect the view of the worksheet such that specified rows and columns remain on the screen, whilst others scroll up and down, left and right as usual. The first technique you will be shown in this chapter is how to fill cells very quickly using a method called *Fill By Example*.

8.3 Filling a range of cells by example

There are some instances where Excel can fill the cells in your worksheet for you by recognising that the values you have typed in so far are part of a series. For example, if you type 1991, 1992 and 1993 into three adjacent cells and select the next nine cells, Excel will fill them with 1994 to 2002.

1. Start **Excel**, then create a new worksheet identical to Figure 8.1. You will need to widen column **A**.

	A	B	C
1	SALES FIGURES FOR YEAR		
2			
3			
4	Project Sales		
5	Actual Sales		
6	5% Commission		
7			
8	Net Sales		
9			
10	% Sales Achieved		
11	Next Months Sales		

Figure 8.1 Fill by example worksheet

2. Type **Jan** into cell **B3**. Notice that the selection border around the cell has a small box on the bottom right corner. Refer to Figure 8.2.

Figure 8.2 Selected cell

3. Position the mouse pointer above that corner, then click and drag to cover cells **C3** to **M3**. The months **Feb** to **Dec** will be inserted.

B	C	D	E	F	G	H	I	J	K	L	M
FOR YEAR											
Jan	Feb	Mar	Apr	May	Jun	Jul	Aug	Sep	Oct	Nov	Dec

Figure 8.3 Fill by example months Feb to Dec

*Q1.   Click and the drag the bottom right corner of cell **M3** to cover cells
N3 to **P3**. What happens? Use **Edit** and **Clear** to clear N3 to P3.*

4.   **Save** the workbook on **floppy disk** under the name **Yearsales** and
Close it. Stay in Excel.

8.4   Using formulae

One of the main advantages of a spreadsheet tool, such as Excel, is that you
can carry out calculations upon the values in a worksheet referring to the cell
addresses rather than the values in the cell. Cell **C3** for example, could contain a formula =**A3** + **B3**. The value displayed in cell **C3** would be the contents of **A3** and **B3** added together. If the value in cell **A3** changed, the resulting value in cell **C3** would be changed automatically. A formula must begin with a mathematical symbol, such as = and can contain numbers, cell addresses and + to add, - to subtract, / to divide or * to multiply.

1.   Open workbook **Saleswb3** on your **floppy disk.** Make cell **B11** current
and click the = on the **Editing Bar**. An = sign will be inserted into the
formula bar. Refer to Figure 8.4.

Figure 8.4 Editing bar and formula bar

Version 7   The **Editing Bar** will be slightly different to Figure 8.4 and
will not display a **Formula Result** box below it. Click the
Formula Bar and type an = sign.

2.   Type the following formula into the **Formula Bar**:

B6+B7+B8+B9+B10

Notice that as you type the formula, it appears in cell **B11** and the result of the formula is displayed in the **Formula result** box below the **Editing Bar**. When you have completed the formula, click the **Tick** box. Refer to Figure 8.5.

SUM	▼	X	✓	=	=B6+B7+B8+B9+B10

?	Formula result = £		807.00	OK	Cancel

5	Actual Sales:					
6	Speakers	£ 350.00	£ 605.00	£ 560.00	£ 300.00	£ 75.00
7	Headsets	£ 200.00	£ 210.00	£ 120.00	£ 40.00	£ 620.00
8	Sockets	£ 97.00	£ 15.00	£ 25.00	£ 175.00	£ 140.00
9	Fuses	£ 45.00	£ 25.00	£ 125.00	£ 160.00	£ 75.00
10	Cables	£ 115.00	£ 20.00	£ 210.00	£ 230.00	£ 135.00
11	Total Sales	39+B10				

Figure 8.5 Completed formula

Q2. *How do cells **B10** and **B11** differ in respect of what is displayed in the cell and the **Formula Bar** for each cell?*

3. Change the formula by making cell **B11** current again, then clicking the = in the **Editing Bar**.

Version 7 Make **B11** current and click the **Formula Bar** on the **Editing Bar**.

4. Amend the formula by deleting **+B10**. If you wanted to accept the change, you would click **OK** or the **Tick** box, but in this case, click the **Cross** to return to the previous formula.

5. Fill cells **C11** to **F11**, referred to as range **C11:F11,** by first making cell **B11** current, then clicking and dragging the bottom right corner of the cell to cover cells **C11:F11**. You may need to widen column **D** to fit the total. Refer to Figure 8.6.

3		Sarah	Tony	Emily	David	Rachel	Totals
4	Projected Sales	£ 850.00	£ 1,500.00	£ 920.00	£ 650.00	£ 1,000.00	
5	Actual Sales:						
6	Speakers	£ 350.00	£ 605.00	£ 560.00	£ 300.00	£ 75.00	
7	Headsets	£ 200.00	£ 210.00	£ 120.00	£ 40.00	£ 620.00	
8	Sockets	£ 97.00	£ 15.00	£ 25.00	£ 175.00	£ 140.00	
9	Fuses	£ 45.00	£ 25.00	£ 125.00	£ 160.00	£ 75.00	
10	Cables	£ 115.00	£ 20.00	£ 210.00	£ 230.00	£ 135.00	
11	Total Sales	£ 807.00	£ 875.00	£ 1,040.00	£ 905.00	£ 1,045.00	

Figure 8.6 Fill By example formulae

6. Make cell **C11** current. You will see the formula

=**C6+C7+C8+C9+C10** displayed in the **Formula Bar**.

When Excel is used to fill, copy or move a formula in this way, Excel will change the addresses in the formula relative to the distance from the original cell. For example, when the contents of cell **B11** were copied into cell **C11** using the **Fill By Example** method, the address of the new cell **C11** is one column higher than **B11**. The row is the same. Therefore, all addresses in the formula are increased by one column. All the **B** parts of the addresses became **C**. In cell **F11**, all **B** parts of the addresses in the formula were increased by four columns to **F** addresses. Hence addresses such as **A10** and **F26** are called **Relative Addresses**.

7. Make cell **B12** current and click the = on the **Editing Bar**.

Version 7   Make **B12** current. Click the **Formula Bar** and type an = sign.

8. **Type** the formula **(5/100)*B11**. Click the **Tick** box.

You must be careful when using formulae where there is more than one mathematical operation being performed to use brackets to ensure that the mathematical operations will be applied in the correct order. The part of the formula within the brackets will be performed first. For example, the formula 5+10*2 gives the result 25 since, unless there are brackets, Excel will always perform the * or / operations before a + or -, whereas the formula (5+10)*2 gives the result 30.

9. This time, copy cell **B12** into range **C12:F12** by making **B12** current, then click the **Copy** icon, then select the range **C12:F12** and click the **Paste** icon. Press the **Esc** key to remove the copy selection.

Q3. What is the formula in cell D12?

10. Using the same procedures as above, type formula = **B11-B12** into cell **B13** and fill cells **C13:F13** as before. Apply the **Style Currency** format to cells **B12:G13**. Refer to Figure 8.7.

11. Use the click and drag method to widen column **A** to fit the **% Sales Achieved** text in cell **A15**.

12. To show the Total Sales as a percentage of Projected Sales, make cell **B15** current and type the following formula following the above procedures = **B11/B4**

13. To turn this formula into a percentage, ensure **B15** is still current and click the **Percent Style** icon **%** on the formatting bar. Copy **B15** into cells **C15:F15** using the **Fill By Example** method. Refer to Figure 8.7.

14. **Save** the workbook **Saleswb3**.

3		Sarah	Tony	Emily	David	Rachel	Totals
4	Projected Sales	£650.00	£1,500.00	£ 920.00	£650.00	£1,000.00	£ 4,920.00
5	Actual Sales:						
6	Speakers	£350.00	£ 605.00	£ 560.00	£300.00	£ 75.00	
7	Headsets	£200.00	£ 210.00	£ 120.00	£ 40.00	£ 620.00	
8	Sockets	£ 97.00	£ 15.00	£ 25.00	£175.00	£ 140.00	
9	Fuses	£ 45.00	£ 25.00	£ 125.00	£160.00	£ 75.00	
10	Cables	£115.00	£ 20.00	£ 210.00	£230.00	£ 135.00	
11	Total Sales	£807.00	£ 875.00	£ 1,040.00	£905.00	£1,045.00	
12	5% Commission	£ 40.35	£ 43.75	£ 52.00	£ 45.25	£ 52.25	
13	Net Sales	£766.65	£ 831.25	£ 988.00	£859.75	£ 992.75	
14							
15	% Sales Achieved	95%	58%	113%	139%	105%	

Figure 8.7 Completed formulae

8.5 Using functions

You have already seen how formulae are used to carry out calculations in a worksheet. The most commonly used formulae have been given names to match their type of calculation so that they can be used easily. The **SUM** function, for example, adds up the contents of a range of cell addresses. =SUM(B6:B10) adds up the values in cells **B6** to **B10**, in the same way as the current formula in cell **B11** does, =B6+B7+B8+B9+B10. Since function names are predefined in Excel, you do not need to type the name of function, you can select it from a list. You will then be asked to enter the range you wish your function to apply to.

Version 7 There are a few differences between the Function Wizard in Version 97 and Version 7 of Excel. If you have Version 7, omit steps 1 to 5 and follow the Version 7 instructions provided after step 5.

1. Make cell **G4** current and click the = on the **Editing Bar**.

2. Click the **down scroll arrow** next to the **Name Box**. A list of functions

will be displayed. Assume you want a function not in the list, so click **More Functions**. The following window will be displayed as show in Figure 8.8.

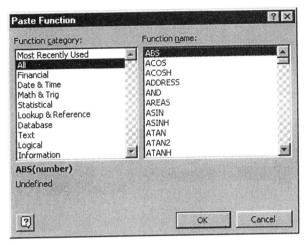

Figure 8.8 Paste Function Window

3. Click **Math & Trig** in the **Function category** list. The functions in that category will be displayed in the **Function name** window.

Q4. What are the top four Math & Trig functions?

4. Click the **Most Recently Used** category, then the **SUM** function name and click **OK**.

5. Excel has assumed that you wish to apply the function to the range **B4:F4**. This is correct, but if this was not the case, you could simply overwrite the range with the correct range. The result of the **SUM** on the range is shown at the bottom of the window. Click **OK**. Refer to Figure 8.9.

Version 7   1. Make **G4** current and click the **Formula Bar**.
         2. Click the **Function Wizard** *f∗* on the **Editing Bar**.
         3. Click **Math & Trig** in the **Function category** list. The functions in that category will be displayed in the **Function name** window.
         4. Click **Most Recently Used** category, then click the **SUM** function name. Click the **Next** box.
         5. Type the cell range **B4:F4** into the **number 1** box. Click the **Finish** box, then click the **Tick** box in the **Editing Bar**.

Functions and formulae   95

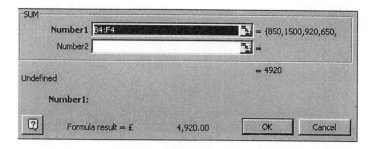

Figure 8.9 SUM Function

6.   You may need to widen column **G** using the click and drag method.

If you want to add up two different ranges of cells, for example, **B4:F4** and **B6:F6**, you would type the second range in the **Number 2** box giving the SUM function =SUM(B4:F4,B6:F6).

Another way to insert a function into a cell is to make the cell current, then click the **Paste Function** icon f_x on the toolbar. The **Paste Function** window will appear, as in Figure 8.8, and you can continue to select and define your function as above.

Version 7   The f_x icon is called the **Function Wizard** icon.

A quick way to use the **SUM** function is to use the **Autosum** button on the toolbar by selecting the cell you want the function inserted into, then click the **Autosum** button. Excel will assume you want to add up the values in the previous numerical cells in the row or column and insert the **SUM** function for that range in the cell. You can alter the range.

7.   Make cell **G6** current, then click the **Autosum** icon Σ. The **SUM** function for range of cells **B6:F6** will be inserted into cell **G6** and cells **B6:F6** will be outlined in a flashing border. Refer to Figure 8.10. Press **enter.**

8.   Use the **Fill By Example** method to copy cell **G6** onto cells **G7:G13.**

If you needed to select a non-continuous range of cells, G7:G13 and G15 for example, you would select the first range, G7:G13, then hold the Ctrl key down whilst you select the second range, cell G15. Release the Ctrl key.

9.   **Save** the worksheet **Saleswb3** on your floppy disk.

3		Sarah	Tony	Emily	David	Rachel	Totals
4	Projected Sales	£850.00	£1,500.00	£ 920.00	£650.00	£1,000.00	
5	Actual Sales:						
6	Speakers	£350.00	£ 605.00	£ 560.00	£300.00	£ 75.00	=SUM(B6:F6)
7	Headsets	£200.00	£ 210.00	£ 120.00	£ 40.00	£ 620.00	1R x 5C
8	Sockets	£ 97.00	£ 15.00	£ 25.00	£175.00	£ 140.00	

Figure 8.10 Autosum function tool

8.6 Using absolute cell addresses

You have already seen how, when you copy the formula in a cell into another cell, the address changes relative to the distance between the original and the new cell. This type of cell address, **B6** for example, is called a *Relative* cell address. To stop a cell address being altered when being copied, insert a dollar sign before the row and column addresses in a formula, **$B$6** for example. This type of address is called an *Absolute* cell address.

The formulae in the cells in row **12** calculate the 5% commission on the Total Sales value. The formula in **B12** is =(5/100)*B11. The drawback with this calculation is that if the commission percentage should change, all the formulae in row 12 will need to be changed. Amend the worksheet such that the commission is a value in a cell rather than a number in a formula:

1. Enter the text **Commission %** in cell **A2** and enter the formula =5/100 in cell **B2**. Apply the **Percentage Style** to cell **B2**.

2. Edit cell **A12** to remove the text **5%**, leaving only the word **Commission** and clear down cells **B12:F12** by selecting the cells then using the **Edit, Clear** and **Contents** commands or pressing the **Delete** key. If you cleared **All**, the currency format would also be lost.

3. Enter the formula =$B$2 *B11 into cell **B12**, then **Fill By Example** cells **C12:F12** from cell **B12**. Refer to Figure 8.11.

Q5. What is the formula in E12?

4. **Save** you workbook **Saleswb3**.

3		Sarah	Tony	Emily	David	Rachel	Totals
4	Projected Sales	£850.00	£1,500.00	£ 920.00	£650.00	£1,000.00	£ 4,920.00
5	Actual Sales:						
6	Speakers	£350.00	£ 605.00	£ 560.00	£300.00	£ 75.00	£ 1,890.00
7	Headsets	£200.00	£ 210.00	£ 120.00	£ 40.00	£ 620.00	£ 1,190.00
8	Sockets	£ 97.00	£ 15.00	£ 25.00	£175.00	£ 140.00	£ 452.00
9	Fuses	£ 45.00	£ 25.00	£ 125.00	£160.00	£ 75.00	£ 430.00
10	Cables	£115.00	£ 20.00	£ 210.00	£230.00	£ 135.00	£ 710.00
11	Total Sales	£807.00	£ 875.00	£ 1,040.00	£905.00	£1,045.00	£ 4,672.00
12	5% Commission	£ 40.35	£ 43.75	£ 52.00	£ 45.25	£ 52.25	£ 233.60

Figure 8.11 Commission formulae with absolute cell address

8.7 Freezing panes on the screen

If you were asked to enter Bonus Payment values in row 28 of your worksheet, you would have trouble working out to whom the expenses referred
because the names at the top of the columns would be on the previous screen.
Try it out. One way to keep certain rows or columns from moving, no matter
how much you scroll the worksheet up, down or across, is to *Freeze the Panes*
on the screen.

1. Enter the text **Bonus Payments** in cell **A28**, then make cell **B4** current,
    then click **Window** and **Freeze Panes**. A line will appear above the
    current cell and to the left of the current cell.

2. Scroll down the screen. Watch the top three rows remain on the screen,
    whilst the others scroll. Scroll to the right also. Scroll down to view row
    28 on the screen and enter the values shown in Figure 8.12 for cells
    C28 and **F28**. Apply the currency style to range **B28:F28**.

3. Remove the frozen panes by clicking **Window** and **Unfreeze Panes**,
    then close workbook **Saleswb3** without saving it and close Excel.

	A	B	C	D	E	F	G
1	JANUARY SALES FIGURES						
2	Commission	5%					
3		Sarah	Tony	Emily	David	Rachel	Totals
27							
28	Bonus Payments		£ 95.00			£ 110.00	

Figure 8.12 Freezing panes

In this chapter, you will have been shown how to do the following:

- Fill a range by example by **clicking** and **dragging** the bottom right corner of the current cell.
- Create formulae using the **Edit Line** and **Formula Bar**.
- Use functions to carry out commonly used formulae, using the **Name Box** on the **Edit Line,** the **Paste Function** or **Autosum** icons on the toolbar.
- Use absolute cell addresses in formulae and functions to stop the address being altered when being copied, buy inserting dollar signs.
- Freeze Panes on the screen by clicking the **Window, Freeze Panes** commands and **Window, Unfreeze Panes** commands to remove them.

8.9   Written exercises

8.9.1   Write down the following functions and formulae, for the worksheet in Figure 8.13:

(a) The formula in **B4** = Five times the year in **B3**.
The function in **B8** = Total of cells **B4:B7**
The function in **E4** = Total of cells **B4:D4.**
The function in **F4** = Average value of cells **B4:D4.**

(b) Explain how to use the Fill by Example method to fill cells **C8** and **D8** from cell **B8**, to fill cells **E5** to **E8** from cell **E4**, and finally to fill cells **F5** to **F8** from cell **F4**. Note that the function in cell **F8** represents the average of the totals in cells **B8, C8** and **D8**, not the total of the averages in column **F**.

A	B	C	D	E	F
1	Annual Income Report				
2					
3		1994	1995	1996	Total	Average
4 Basic Salary	£ 9,970.00	£ 9,975.00	£ 9,980.00	£29,925.00	£ 9,975.00
5 Commission	£ 5,500.00	£ 6,000.00	£ 6,700.00	£18,200.00	£ 6,066.67
6 Consultancy	£ 950.00	£ 1,200.00	£ 2,500.00	£ 4,650.00	£ 1,550.00
7 Bonus Payments	£ 250.00	£ 200.00	£ 150.00	£ 600.00	£ 200.00
8 Annual Total	£ 16,670.00	£17,375.00	£19,330.00	£53,375.00	£17,791.67
9					

Figure 8.13 Annual Income Report

8.9.2 The worksheet in Figure 8.13 has been amended to include four additional rows; 3, 4, 11 and 14. Refer to Figure 8.14:

	A	B	C	D	E	F
1		Annual Income Report				
2						
3	Annual Savings Interest	£ 350.00				
4	Royalty per Book	£ 0.40				
5						
6		1994	1995	1996	Total	Average
7	Basic Salary	£ 9,970.00	£ 9,975.00	£ 9,980.00	£ 29,925.00	£ 9,975.00
8	Commission	£ 5,500.00	£ 6,000.00	£ 6,700.00	£ 18,200.00	£ 6,066.67
9	Consultancy	£ 950.00	£ 1,200.00	£ 2,500.00	£ 4,650.00	£ 1,550.00
10	Bonus Payments	£ 250.00	£ 200.00	£ 150.00	£ 600.00	£ 200.00
11	Book Royalties	£ 1,000.00	£ 900.00	£ 700.00	£ 2,600.00	£ 866.67
12	Annual Total	£ 18,020.00	£ 18,625.00	£ 20,380.00	£ 57,025.00	£ 19,008.33
13						
14	Number Books Sold	2500	2250	1750		
15						

Figure 8.14 Amended Annual Income Report

Write down the functions and formulae for the amended cells:

(a) The formula in **B11** = Royalty Payment in **B4** multiplied by the value in cell **B14**. The formula should be written such that it can be copied to cells **C11** and **D11** without address **B4** changing.

(b) The formula in **B12** = Total of cells **B7:B11** plus the value in cell **B3**. The formula should be written such that it can be copied to cells **C12** and **D12**, without address **B3** changing.

8.10 Practical exercises

8.10.1 Use Excel to create a new workbook called **AnIncRep1** on your floppy disk and complete the worksheet in Figure 8.14 according to the instructions given in exercises 8.9.1 and 8.9.2.

8.10.2 Retrieve the **Persbudg3** workbook from your floppy disk created in the previous chapter. Use appropriate functions and formulae to complete the **Total Income, Total Expenses** and **Net Income** rows, and the **Total** column on the right of the worksheet. Save the workbook under the same name.

8.10.3 Retrieve the **Finanrep1** workbook used in the previous two chapters and complete it as follows, then save under the same name:

(a) Using appropriate functions and formulae, complete the **Total**

Income, Total Expenses and **Net Income** rows. Using the **Autosum** icon, complete the **Total** column.

(b) Enter a formula into cell **F5** to calculate the Total Fees as a percentage of the Total Income for the quarter (Total Fees/Total Income). Use the **Percent Style** icon to convert the fraction into a percentage. Then Fill by Example cell **F6** from cell **F5.**

(c) Enter a formula into cell **F11** to calculate the Total Salaries as a percentage of the Total Expenses for the quarter. Use the **Percent Style** icon to convert the fraction into a percentage. Then Fill by Example cells **F12** and **F13** from cell **F11**.

9 Microsoft Excel – Charts and Multi-Worksheet Workbooks

9.1 Overview

In this chapter you will learn how to carry out the following techniques:

- Create a chart.
- Preview and print a chart.
- Amend chart features.
- Create a multi-series chart.
- Insert a chart into a Word document.
- Use more than one worksheet in a workbook.
- Link worksheets together.
- Add headers, footers and page numbers to a workbook.

9.2 Introduction

You have already been shown how to create a worksheet and how to use functions, formulae and absolute cell addresses to manipulate and complete the information on a worksheet. Once this information has been recorded in the worksheet, it can be illustrated as a graph or *chart*. Excel provides a *Chart Wizard* to assist you. The Chart Wizard will need to be told which areas of your worksheet should be used as the data and for labels for the axes, as well as which type of chart you require. Once the chart has been created, it can easily be amended in Excel and copied into a word document.

It is also possible to use more than one worksheet in a workbook and to link them together by referring to a cell address in another worksheet. In this way, you could create a workbook, for example, containing five worksheets of data. The first four worksheets containing Sales figures for each of the four quarters of the year, and the fifth worksheet containing the total of the four quarters' figures. You will also be shown how to insert page numbers, headers and footers on your worksheets.

To create a graph or *chart* in Excel, you must first specify the range of cells to be used in the chart, including appropriate column and row headings. You then invoke the Chart Wizard which displays a series of windows or *steps* asking you to confirm or amend information used to construct the chart.

1.   Start Excel and insert your floppy disk. Retrieve the workbook **Saleswb3** from the floppy disk and using **File**, **Save As** save it under a new name **Saleswb3chart**.

Version 7   There are several differences between the Chart Wizard in Version 97 and version 7 of Excel. If you have Version 7, omit steps 2–12 and follow the Version 7 instructions provided after step 12.

2.   Select cell range **A3:F4**. Click **Insert**, then click **Chart**.

3.   The **Chart Wizard – Step 1 of 4 – Chart Type** window is displayed. Refer to Figure 9.1. This window allows you to select which type of chart you require, and shows you what your chart will look like for each type. Click Chart Type of **Line**, then click and hold the mouse button on the **Press and hold to view sample** box. A preview of your chart as a line chart will be shown. Reselect **Column** and click **Next**.

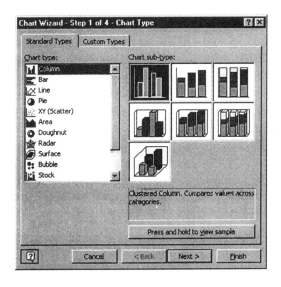

Figure 9.1 Chart Wizard – Step 1 of 4 – Chart Type

4. The **Chart Wizard – Step 2 of 4 – Chart Source Data** window is displayed. Refer to Figure 9.2. This window allows you to confirm the range of cells used as data for the chart. In this chart, the range includes the heading row 3 and the heading column A, as well as the projected sales values in row 4. The **Series** has been specified as **Rows** which means that the values plotted against the x-axis, are assumed to be values in the same series, row 4.

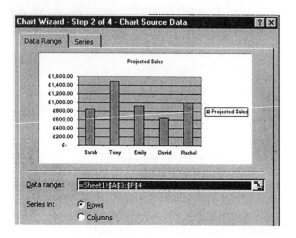

Figure 9.2 Chart Wizard – Step 2 of 4 – Chart Source Data

5. Click the **Series** tab heading. This window allows you to confirm which parts of the cell range are to be used when defining the series in the chart. The **Name** box correctly shows the range of the cells containing the name of the series, **Projected Sales**. The **Values** box correctly shows the range of cells to be used as the values in the series. Click **Next**.

6. The **Chart Wizard – Step 3 of 4 – Chart Options** window will be displayed. Refer to Figure 9.3.

    This window allows you to specify various layout and textual settings for your chart. Change the **Chart title** box to **Projected Sales for January 1997** and type **Sales Staff** into the **Category (X) axis** box.

7. Click the **Axes** tab heading. Click the **Value (Y) axis** box removing the tick. Watch the preview change. Reselect the box.

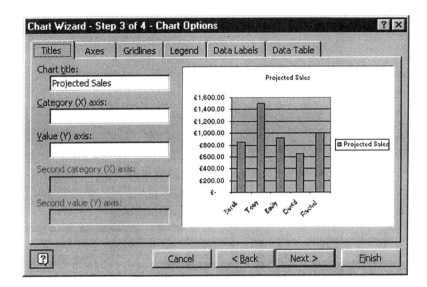

Figure 9.3 Chart Wizard – Step 3 of 4 – Chart Options

Q1. What happened to the preview when the tick was removed?

8. Click the **Gridlines** tab heading to view the Gridlines window. Click the **Major Gridlines** box in the **Category (X) axis** section. Watch the preview change. Click the box again to remove the tick.

Q2. What happens when you select Major X axis Gridlines?

9. Click the **Legend** tab heading to view the Legend window. Click the **legend** box to remove the tick and watch the preview change. Reselect the **Legend** box.

Q3. What happens when you removed the legend tick?

10. Click the **Data Labels** tab heading to view the data labels window. Click against **Show Value**. The corresponding value from the worksheet is shown above each column. Select **Show Label**. Watch the preview change, then select **None**.

Q4. What happens when you select Show Label?

11. Click the **Data Table** tab heading to view the data table window. Click the **Show Data Table** box and the values from the worksheet will appear under the chart in a table. Click the box again to remove the tick. Click **Next**.

12.   The **Chart Wizard – Step 4 of 4 – Chart Location** window will be displayed. This window allows you to specify whether you want the chart to be placed in a new worksheet in your workbook, or in an existing worksheet. Leave the selection as **Sheet1**. Click **Finish**.

Version 7 begin

1.   Select cell range **A3:F4**. Click **Insert**, then point to **Chart**. Click on **On This Sheet**. A + sign with a small icon of a chart will appear. Scroll down to below the table and click and drag the + sign to form a large rectangle.

3.   Step 1 of 5. Click **Next** to accept the range =**$A$3:$F$4**

4.   Step 2 of 5. Select the chart type **Column**. Click **Next**.

5.   Step 3 of 5. Select column format type number **6** if not already selected. Click **Next**.

6.   Step 4 of 5. A sample chart will be shown. Refer to Figure 9.2. The series is specified as Rows. Select **Columns** and watch the sample chart change.

7.   Reselect **Rows**. Click **Next** to confirm the first row and column are to be used as x-axis and legend text.

8.   Step 5 of 5. Type **Projected Sales for January 1997** into the **Title** box and type **Sales Staff** into the **Category (X)** box. Click **Finish**.

Version 7 end

13.   The chart will be inserted in your worksheet. You may need to click and drag the worksheet chart to appear below the table. You may also need to click and drag the top or bottom edges of the chart border to enlarge the chart area to be able to see the chart clearly. Refer to Figure 9.4. The values shown on the y-axis may differ, depending on the size of your chart.

14.   Save the workbook, **Saleswb3chart**.

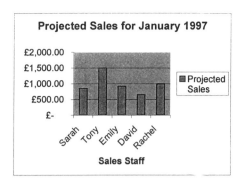

Figure 9.4 Chart produced using the Chart Wizard

<hr>

9.4 Preview and print a chart

Printing a chart is similar to printing a worksheet, except that you must first select the chart before you can specify the printing options required.

1. Double-click anywhere inside the outer edge of the chart to select the chart. The chart will have a shaded outline border once selected.

2. Click the **Print Preview** icon to see what the printed chart will look like. Click the **Print** box at the top of the window. The **Print** window will be displayed. Click **OK**.

Instead of clicking the **Print** box at the top of the **Print Preview** window, you could have clicked **Close** on the preview and either clicked the **Print** icon on the toolbar for the default print or clicked **File** and **Print** from the menu bar.

<hr>

9.5 Amending chart features

Once a chart has been selected, any of the features set up for the chart using the Chart Wizard can be amended using the Chart command on the menu bar. The pull-down menu for this menu option lists the four Chart Wizard steps by name: Chart Type, Source Data, Chart Options and Location. By selecting any of these, you can amend any of the windows previously displayed as part of the initial Chart Wizard.

Version 7 The **Chart** menu option is not available in *Version 7*. However, the features of the chart can be amended using the **Insert** and **Format** menu options as well as the **Chart** toolbar, which can be selected using the **View, Toolbars** menu options. Omit steps 1 and 2 below, and carry out the *Version 7* actions shown below step 2.

1.   Select the chart and click **Chart** on the menu bar. A pull-down menu will appear. Click **Chart Options**. Click the **Titles** tab heading. Change the title of the **Category (X) Axis** from **Sales Staff** to **Sales Executives**.

2.   Click the **Gridlines** tab heading. Click the box next to the **Major Gridlines** under the **Category (X) Axis**. Click the remaining tab headings in turn to view the window for each. Finally, click **OK**.

Version 7 Double-click inside the chart border to select it, then single-click the **Sales Staff** title. Type **Sales Executives** into the **Formula Bar**. Click the **tick**. Click **Insert**, then **Gridlines**. Click the box next to **Major Gridlines** under the **Category (X) Axis**. Click **OK**.

You can also change the features of a chart directly using the mouse pointer to select the feature, then changing it.

3.   Click anywhere on the chart's title to select it. The text **Chart Title** will appear in the **Name Box** on the **Editing Bar**.

4.   Use the mouse pointer to position the cursor at the left of the word **for**. Delete it using the **Delete key** on the keyboard and replace it with a hyphen -. Click in the middle of the chart to confirm the change.

The range of cells upon which the chart is based are still linked to the chart. If the value in one of the cells changes, the chart will be automatically updated to reflect this change.

5.   Make cell **E3** current and change the text from **David** to **Daniel**. Scroll down to see that the chart will also have been changed.

6.   Make cell **F4** current and change the amount from **£1000.00** to **£1750.00**. Again, scroll down to see that the chart will also have been changed. Refer to Figure 9.5.

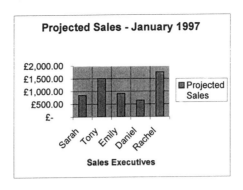

Figure 9.5 Amended chart

7.   Save the workbook, **Saleswb3chart**.

To create a chart to show two or more series of numbers, use the **Chart Wizard** as before, but select more than one row or column of numbers to be included in the chart. You are going to create a chart to show a comparison between the Actual Sales figures for Sarah and Tony. In this example, there are two series of numbers in columns, one for Sarah and one for Tony. Since the row containing the column or series headings is not next to the cells with the data, you will need to select the split cell range using the **Ctrl** key:

1.   Select the range **A3:C3**, then hold the **Ctrl** key on the keyboard down and select the range **A6:C10**. Release the **Ctrl** key.

Version 7   If you have *Version 7,* omit steps 2 – 5, and carry out the *Version 7* instructions provided after step 5.

2.   Click the **Insert Chart** icon. Click **Next** on step 1 of 4 .

3.   In the **Step 2 of 4** window, click the circle against **Columns**. Watch the preview change. Click **Next**.

4.   In the **Step 3 of 4** window, enter a **Chart Title** of **Actual Sales – Sarah and Tony** and a title on the X axis of **Actual Sales**. Click **Next** on this window.

5.   In the **step 4 of 4** window, click **Finish**.

Charts and multisheet workbooks   109

Version 7   Click the **Chart Wizard** icon and click and drag the + sign below the previous chart to form a large rectangle. Click **Next** on steps 1, 2, 3 and 4. Type a chart title of **Actual Sales – Sarah and Tony** and an x-axis title of **Actual Sales.** Click **Finish**.

6.   The chart will be inserted into the worksheet. You may need to click and drag the chart to below the previous chart and to click and drag the sides of the chart to enlarge it. Refer to Figure 9.6.

7.   Save the workbook, **Saleswb3chart**.

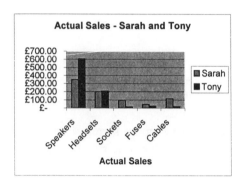

Figure 9.6 Multi-series chart

9.7   Inserting a chart into a Word document

It is often useful to be able to copy a chart produced using Excel, into a Word document. To insert any section of worksheet or chart from one worksheet to another, or into a Word document, you simply select the range of cells or chart, then click **Copy**. You then position the cursor where you wish the copied item to be inserted, and click **Paste**.

1.   Double-click anywhere on the chart you have just created to select it. Then click the **Copy** icon. Click the **Application Minimise** button ![button] at the top right hand corner of the screen to reduce **Excel** to a button on the taskbar.

2.   **Open** Word and type the following text into the empty document displayed: **The following chart illustrates the Actual Sales Figures for January 1997 of Tony Miles and Sarah Henderson:**

3. Press **Enter** twice, then click the **Paste** icon. The chart will be inserted into your document. **Save** the document on your floppy disk as **SalesWord1**.

4. **Close** the document **SalesWord1**, then **Close** Word. Click the **Excel** button on the task bar to open the Excel workbook again. **Close** the workbook **Saleswb3chart**.

9.8   Using more than one worksheet in a workbook

So far, you have only used one worksheet in the workbook, **Sheet1**. In some circumstances, you may wish to use several worksheets and link them together. For example, a Sales Report could contain a monthly report for each month in a quarter on worksheets **Sheet1**, **Sheet2** and **Sheet3**, and then combine the figures into a quarterly report on **Sheet4**. You would usually create the same basic table structure on each worksheet by making all four worksheets current before creating the table. However, since you have already created sheet1, you will create three copies of sheet1, before renaming them.

1. Retrieve the workbook **Saleswb3** from the floppy disk and using the **File**, **Save As** commands, copy the workbook under a new name on the floppy disk, **Saleswb3multi**.

2. If any of the cells contain # signs, make the appropriate column wider.

3. To make three copies of **Sheet1**, click the **Edit** menu command and click **Move or Copy Sheet**. The **Move or Copy Sheet** pull-down menu will be displayed. This menu allows you to move or copy the current sheet into another workbook, or simply into a specific position in relation to the other worksheets in the current workbook.

4. Select **Sheet2** in the list and click the box next to **Create a Copy**. Click **OK**. A new sheet will be inserted between **Sheet1** and **Sheet2**, called **Sheet1(2)**.

5. Repeat this procedure to create two additional sheets, **Sheet1(3)** and **Sheet1(4)**, in front of **Sheet2**. Refer to Figure 9.7.

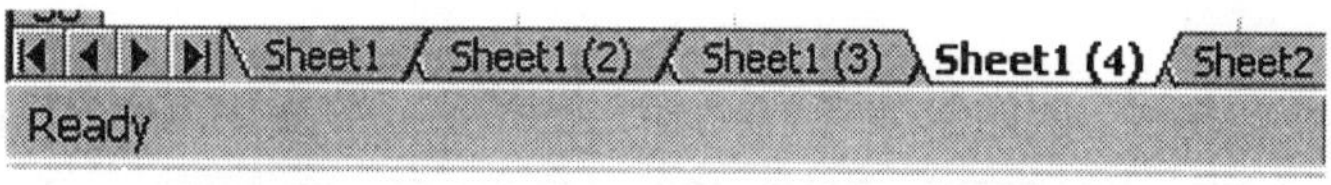

Figure 9.7 Three copied versions of Sheet1

6. Click the **Sheet1** tab to make it current. Rename **Sheet1** by clicking the **Format** menu command, then point to **Sheet**. A pull-down menu will be displayed. Click on **Rename**.

7. Type the text **January** into the **Sheet1** tab. Click anywhere on the worksheet to confirm the change.

Version 7 Type the text **January** into the **Name** box and click **OK**.

8. Repeat this procedure and rename the next three worksheets as **February**, **March** and **Quarter**. Also, change the title of each worksheet in cell **A1** to **February Sales Figures**, **March Sales Figures** and **First Quarter Sales Figures** respectively.

9. Make the **January** worksheet current. Enter the figures **950, 1250, 800, 500** and **900** into cells **B17, C17, D17, E17** and **F17**.

10. To apply the currency style to a range of cells in all four worksheets simultaneously, hold down the **Ctrl** key and click the tabs for worksheets **January, February, March** and **Quarter** to select them in a group. Select cells **B17:F17** and click the **Currency Style** icon. Click the **Sheet2** tab to deselect the group.

9.9   Linking worksheets together

You have already used formulae containing the addresses rather than the values in cells. In the same way, you can refer to the address of a cell in a specific worksheet by prefixing the cell address with the sheet name. Amend the **February** and **March** worksheets such that their **Projected Sales** figures are taken from the previous month's **Next Months Sales** figures.

1. Make the **February** worksheet current. Use the **Edit, Clear** and **Contents** commands to clear cells **B4:F4**. The **% Sales Achieved** cells will show error **#DIV/0!**, which means that the formulae in these cells are being asked to divide by zero. This will be rectified shortly.

2.   Make cell **B4** current and click the = sign in the **Editing Bar**.

Version 7   Make cell **B4** current and click the **Formula Bar**.

3.   Click the **January** worksheet tab. The text **January!** will be shown in the **Formula Bar**. Click cell **B17**. The text **January!B17** will appear in the **Formula Bar**. Click the tick in the **Editing Bar**. The **February** worksheet will become current again.

4.   Still using the **February** worksheet, use the **Fill by Example** method to copy cell **B4** to cells **C4:F4**. Refer to Figure 9.8.

| 4 | Projected Sales | £ 950.00 | £ 1,250.00 | £   800.00 | £ 500.00 | £   900.00 | £ 4,400.00 |

Figure 9.8 February Project Sales figures linked to January Next Months Sales figures

5.   Still in the **February** worksheet, enter the following figures into cells **B17:F17**; 900, 1000, 750, 650 and 1100.

6.   Make the **March** worksheet current. Use the **Edit**, **Clear** and **Contents** commands to clear cells **B4:F4**, then follow steps 2 - 4 to link cells **B4:F4** to the cells **B17:F17** in the **February** worksheet.

The **Quarter** worksheet will show the total of all worksheet amounts.

7.   Make the **Quarter** worksheet current and use the **Edit**, **Clear** and **Contents** commands to clear cells **B4:F10**.

8.   Make cell **B4** current and click the = sign in the **Editing Bar**.

Version 7   Make cell **B4** current and click the **Formula Bar**.

9.   Click the **January** worksheet tab, then click cell **B4**. Type a + sign. Click the **February** worksheet tab, then click cell **B4**. Type a + sign again. Click the **March** worksheet tab, then click cell **B4** again. Click the tick. The formula **=January!B4+February!B4+March!B4** will be displayed in the **Formula Bar** for cell **B4** in the **Quarter** worksheet.

10.   In the **Quarter** worksheet, use the **Fill by Example** method to copy cell **B4** to cells **C4:F4**. You may need to make some columns wider.

11.   Make cell **B4** current and click the **Copy** icon. Select cells **B6:F10** and

click the **Paste** icon, then press the **Esc** key. The Quarter worksheet will be completed. Refer to Figure 9.9.

12.   Save the workbook, **Saleswb3multi**.

	A	B	C	D	E	F	G
	FIRST QUARTER SALES FIGURES						
2	Commission	5%					
3		Sarah	Tony	Emily	David	Rachel	Totals
4	Projected Sales	£2,700.00	£3,750.00	£2,470.00	£1,800.00	£3,750.00	£14,470.00
5	**Actual Sales:**						
6	Speakers	£1,050.00	£1,815.00	£1,680.00	£ 900.00	£ 225.00	£ 5,670.00
7	Headsets	£ 600.00	£ 630.00	£ 360.00	£ 120.00	£1,860.00	£ 3,570.00
8	Sockets	£ 291.00	£ 45.00	£ 75.00	£ 525.00	£ 420.00	£ 1,356.00
9	Fuses	£ 135.00	£ 75.00	£ 375.00	£ 480.00	£ 225.00	£ 1,290.00
10	Cables	£ 345.00	£ 60.00	£ 630.00	£ 690.00	£ 405.00	£ 2,130.00
11	Total Sales	£2,421.00	£2,625.00	£3,120.00	£2,715.00	£3,135.00	£14,016.00
12	5% Commission	£ 121.05	£ 131.25	£ 156.00	£ 135.75	£ 156.75	£ 700.80
13	Net Sales	£2,299.95	£2,493.75	£2,964.00	£2,579.25	£2,978.25	£13,315.20
14							
15	% Sales Achieve	90%	70%	126%	151%	84%	97%
16							

January / February / March \ Quarter /

Figure 9.9 Worksheet containing totals from three other worksheets

---

9.10   Adding headers, footers and page numbers to a worksheet

Use the **Page Setup** menu command to add worksheet headers and footers.

1.   Make the **January** worksheet current. Click the **File** menu command, then click **Page Setup**. Click the **Header/Footer** tab at the top of the overlapping windows. The **Header/Footer** window will be displayed.

2.   Click the **Custom Header** box. Refer to Figure 9.10.

3.   Click the **Left section** box and type the text **Loudest Speakers Ltd**. Click the **Right section** box, then click the **Date** icon. Clear the **Centre Section** box if it is not empty. Click **OK**.

*Q5.   What appears in the **Right Section** box?*

114   *Mastering Microsoft Office*

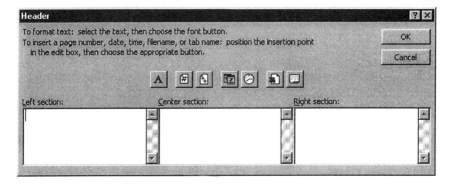

Figure 9.10 Custom Header window

4. Click **Custom Footer**. A window similar to the **Custom Header** window will be displayed. Clear the **Centre Section** box if is it not empty.

    Click the **Right section** box, then click the **Page number** icon ⊞. Click **OK**, then click **OK** again to return to the worksheet. Click the **Print** icon to print the **January** worksheet. Click **OK**. The header and footer will be printed.

5. Save workbook **Saleswb3multi** on floppy disk, then close the workbook and Excel. Remove your floppy disk and **Shut down** the computer.

9.11 Summary

In this chapter, you will have been shown how to do the following:

- Create a chart using the **Chart Wizard**.
- Preview and print a chart by selecting it then using the **Print Preview** and **Print** icons, or using the **File** and **Print** commands.
- Amend chart features by selecting the chart then using the **Chart** menu option or selecting the specific chart feature to amend.
- Create a multi-series chart using the **Chart Wizard**.
- Insert a chart into a Word document using the **Copy** and **Paste** icons.
- Use more than one worksheet in a workbook.
- Link worksheets together by including the worksheet name in a formula.
- Add headers, footers and page numbers using the **Page Setup** and **Header/Footer** commands.

9.12 Written exercises

9.12.1 Write down the range of cells required to create a chart showing the **% Sales Achieved** for each of the five sales staff from the **Quarter** sheet in Figure 9.9. The x-axis and legend titles should be included in the range. Should the series be rows or columns?

9.12.2 What is the cell range required to create a multi-series chart to compare **Projected** and **Total Sales** figures for all five sales staff from the **Quarter** sheet in Figure 9.9. The x-axis and legend titles should be included in the range. Should the series be rows or columns?

9.12.3 A multi-worksheet workbook contains three worksheets: First Phase, Second Phase and Total Effort. The layout, formulae and functions in all three sheets will be the same. **Column C** = Contingency level * Effort column. **Column D** = Effort column + Contingency column. The **Effort** column will differ in each sheet. Refer to Figure 9.11 for the first two sheets. The **Effort** column in the third sheet will contain formulae adding together the corresponding **Effort** values of the first and second worksheets. What are the formulae in cells **B6, C6** and **D6** in the third worksheet?

	A	B	C	D
1	First Phase - Effort Required (person/day)			
2				
3	Contigency level:		20%	
4				
5	Task	Effort	Contigency	Total
6	Task 1.1	2	0.4	2.4
7	Task 1.2	3	0.6	3.6
8	Task 2.1	1.5	0.3	1.8
9	Task 2.2	2.5	0.5	3
10	Task 2.3	7	1.4	8.4
11	Task 3.1	3	0.6	3.6
12	Total	19	3.8	22.8

	A	B	C	D
1	Second Phase - Effort Required (person/day)			
2				
3	Contigency level:		20%	
4				
5	Task	Effort	Contigency	Total
6	Task 1.1	10	2	12
7	Task 1.2	15	3	18
8	Task 2.1	21.5	4.3	25.8
9	Task 2.2	11.5	2.3	13.8
10	Task 2.3	16	3.2	19.2
11	Task 3.1	23	4.6	27.6
12	Total	97	19.4	116.4

Figure 9.11 First and second worksheets

9.13 Practical exercises

9.13.1 Using the worksheet produced in the previous charter, **AnIncRep1**, produce a multi-series chart to show the two series **Commission** and **Consultancy** income figures for the three years 1994, 1995 and 1996. (y-axis = £, x-axis = Years). The chart should be inserted below the Annual Income Report table in the worksheet.

9.13.2   Create the multi-worksheet workbook named **TwoPhasedScheme** described in exercise 9.12.3.

10 Introduction to Databases

10.1 Overview

In this chapter you will create a small database in Access, and perform some simple manipulation on it. You will cover the following features of Access:

- Creating a database.
- Creating a table.
- Entering data.
- Sorting.
- Simple filters.
- Closing a database.

10.2 Introduction

The simplest kind of database consists of a single table of related information. For example, Figure 10.1 shows a table that might be used by a manufacturing organisation to store information about the suppliers of its raw materials. This table could be stored on computer as a database.

Supplier ID	Supplier Name	Address	City	Country
1	Simpsons	East Gate	Oxford	UK
2	Jacksons	West End	Cambridge	UK
3	Cartiers	Les Halles	Paris	France
4	Seidels	Das Haus	Cologne	Germany
5	Scotts	The Green	Manchester	UK
6	Jacksons	Old Yard	Oxford	UK

Figure 10.1 Suppliers table

This table only contains limited information about six suppliers, but a typical organisation may wish to store details about hundreds of suppliers. One reason for storing a large table of this kind on computer rather than paper is that information can then be extracted from it very quickly and easily. For example, even if the table contained thousands of entries it would still only take seconds to produce a list of all suppliers in a particular country. It is also very easy to manipulate a database table. So for example, the table could be sorted into alphabetical order of Supplier Name, Address, Country or City in an instant. New suppliers can easily be inserted into a database table, and old ones edited or deleted. Databases in large organisations are often shared between many users at the same time, so these have the further advantage that everyone has access to the most up to date information.

There are two design features of the table in Figure 10.1 that make it easy to use. First, the full address of each supplier has been separated into three columns: Address, City and Country. An alternative design would be to enter the full address into one column as shown in Figure 10.2.

Supplier ID	Supplier Name	Address
1	Simpsons	East Gate, Oxford, UK.

Figure 10.2 Alternative table layout

The problem with the design of this second table is that it is now difficult to extract all the suppliers in a given country or city, or to sort the suppliers into alphabetical order of country or city. So, when designing database tables, it is very important to separate each of the important types of information into separate columns. Each column in a table is called a *field*, and each row is called a *record*.

The second useful design feature of the table in Figure 10.1 is the inclusion of the *Supplier ID* column. This column can contain no duplicates, which means that no two rows can have the same Supplier ID. This is not true of any other columns in the table. For example, there are two records in the table with the same supplier name: Jacksons. It is clear that these two records do not represent the same supplier since they have different addresses. The simplest way to extract information about one particular supplier is to refer to it by its unique Supplier ID. The name given to the field that identifies each record in a database uniquely is a *primary key* or *key field*. So the primary key in this table is the Supplier ID field.

10.3 Starting Access

Microsoft Access is a *database management system*. This means that it is a system that allows you to design and create databases in the same way that a word processing package allows you to design and create documents. It is important to understand clearly the difference between a database and a database management system. You will probably have used a database before, to search for information in a library for example. You will probably not have used a database management system to create your own database before.

1.   Click on the **Start** button, then point to the **Programs** icon and click on **Microsoft Access**. Alternatively, double-click on the Access icon . You will see a dialogue box similar to that in Figure 10.3. Normally, you would either open an existing database or create a new one when you see this screen, but first we will examine the Access toolbar.

2.   Click on **Cancel** and the screen will clear to look like that in Figure 10.4. The Access screen contains menus, toolbars and a status bar like any other Windows program. The Help menu is standard too. As usual, you can find out what each toolbar button does by pointing at it with your mouse pointer. Many of the buttons on the Access toolbar are the same as in most Windows programs, but there are some new ones, such as the *Relationships* button.

Q1   *What does the Relationships button look like?*

Figure 10.3 Access start up screen

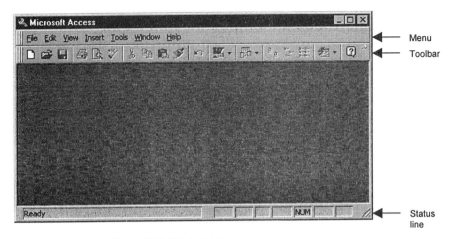

Figure 10.4 Blank database screen

10.4 Creating a new database

1. Click on the **New Database** icon: ☐. The screen will look like that in Figure 10.5.

2. Click on **OK** to see the File New Database dialogue box similar to that in Figure 10.6.

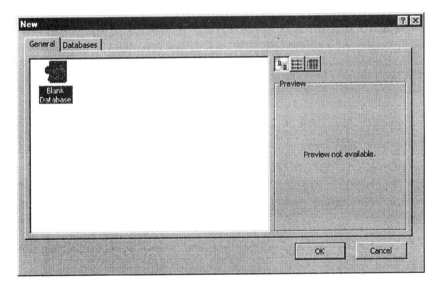

Figure 10.5 New database screen

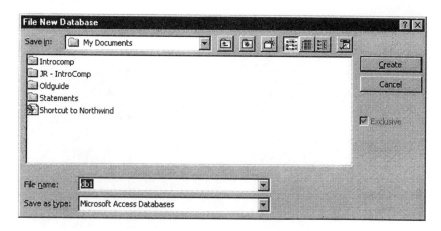

Figure 10.6 File New Database dialogue box

3. Set the **Save in** option to the folder in which you want to save your database, by clicking the down arrow ▼ on the right of the Save in box and selecting an option. If you are using a floppy disk, insert it into the drive and select the **3½ Floppy (A:)** option. You will use this database again in future chapters, so you should put it somewhere accessible.

4. Set the **File name** option to **Shop**, by typing over the default name db1. The extension **mdb** will be added to the filename automatically, so the full name of the database file is **Shop.mdb**, but the extension mdb will not always be displayed.

5. Click on the **Create** button, and you will see the screen in Figure 10.7. You have now created an empty database. The next step will be to create a table of data to work with in the database.

10.5 Creating a table

You will now create the Suppliers table shown in Figure 10.1 at the start of this chapter. The quickest way to create the table is to use the Table Wizard. You will learn about alternative methods later. The Table Wizard is an Access tool that allows you to build tables quickly and easily. There are a number of tables provided by Access for storing commonly used data such as mailing lists, customer details and employee information. You can use the Table Wizard to select one of the built in tables, and then modify it to suit your purpose. The sample tables generally contain a large number of fields, so you will usually only select a small number of the available fields for your table.

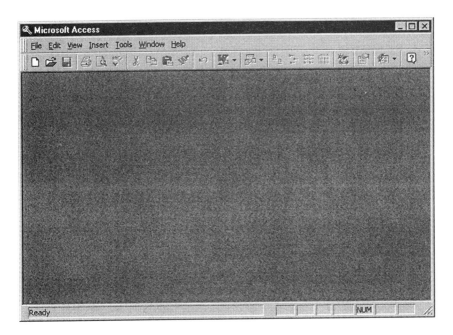

Figure 10.7 Blank database screen

One of the sample tables is called Suppliers and you will use this as a template to construct the Suppliers table shown at the start of this chapter.

1.   Click the **Tables** tab, then click on the **New** button and you will see the New Table dialogue box in Figure 10.8.

2.   Click **Table Wizard** and click **OK**. You will see the Table Wizard dialogue box in Figure 10.9. The column on the left of the table lists all the sample tables designed for business use. There is also a selection of sample tables for personal use. These are displayed when the Personal option at the bottom of the screen is selected. The column in the middle of the screen lists all the fields available in the currently selected table.

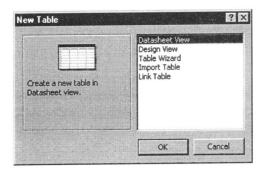

Figure 10.8 New Table dialogue box

In Figure 10.9, the Mailing List table is selected, so the fields shown are some of those that might appear in a standard mailing list. When a different table is selected from the Sample Tables column, a different list of fields will appear in the Sample Fields column. The two uppermost buttons to the right of the Sample Fields column allow you to add fields to the table you create. The ▶ button is for adding a single field, and the ▶▶ button is for adding all the fields.

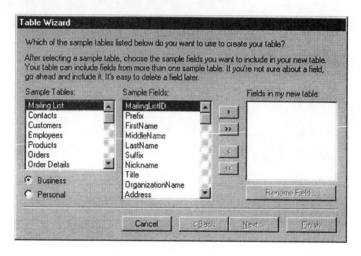

Figure 10.9 Table Wizard dialogue box

3. Scroll down the **Sample Tables** list until you see a table called Suppliers. Select the **Suppliers** table, and a list of fields for that table will appear in the Sample Fields list.

4. Select the **Supplier ID** field if it is not already selected. Click on the Add Field ▶ button. The field will appear in the list headed **Fields in my new table**. If you add the wrong field to your new table by mistake, you can remove it by clicking on the Remove Field ◀ button. Try removing the Supplier ID field and then adding it again.

5. Add the **Supplier Name, Address, City, Country** and **Phone Number** fields to your new table.

6. Click **Next** and you will see the screen in Figure 10.10.

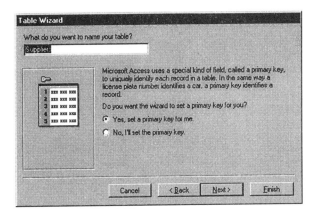

Figure 10.10 Table Wizard finish screen

7. Click **Next** again, to accept the default table name of **Suppliers** and the default option of letting Access set the primary key. All tables created in Access are required to have a primary key. In this case the key will be set to SupplierID automatically. You will now be presented with a choice of three options:

    - Modify the table design.
    - Enter data directly into the table.
    - Enter data into the table using a form the wizard creates for me.

8. Select the second option to enter data directly into the table if it is not already selected, and click **Finish**. You will see the screen in Figure 10.11.

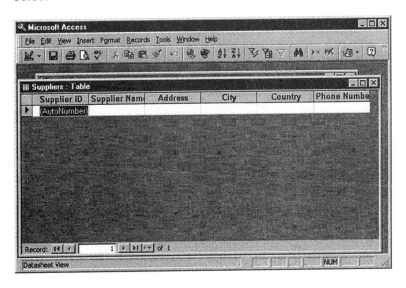

Figure 10.11 Datasheet view of the Suppliers table

There is no need to save the Suppliers table, because Access automatically saves the database whenever you make a change to its structure or data.

Q2 Notice that the toolbar is now different from the original one shown in Figure 10.4. What does the Filter By Selection button look like?

10.6 Entering data

You will now enter the same data into your table as that shown at the start of this chapter. This table is repeated in Figure 10.12.

Supplier ID	SupplierName	Address	City	UK
1	Simpsons	East Gate	Oxford	UK
2	Jacksons	West Gate	Cambridge	UK
3	Cartiers	Les Halles	Paris	UK
4	Seidels	Das Haus	Cologne	Germany
5	Scotts	The Green	Manchester	UK
6	Jacksons	Old Yard	Oxford	UK
(AutoNumber)				

Figure 10.12 Suppliers table

You will not need to enter the numbers into the Supplier ID field, because it has type **AutoNumber**. This means that the numbers will be entered automatically by Access. Follow the instructions below to enter the remaining data.

1. Press the **Tab** key to move past the Supplier ID column to the Supplier Name column and type the first name: **Simpsons**.

2. Press **Tab** again to move to the Address column and type **East Gate**.

3. Continue in this way until you reach the **Country** column. Then press the **Tab** key to move onto the next line.

4. Press **Tab** to move past the Supplier ID column and continue adding all the data shown in Figure 10.12 to the table. The table will be saved automatically by Access.

Q3 Click on the ▌◄ at the bottom of the Suppliers: Table window. How does the screen change?

Most commercial databases contain thousands of different records, rather than the six you have just entered. In such circumstances, it is often useful to sort the data in different ways. You can now experiment with this on your sample table. Follow the steps below to sort the data into ascending order of Supplier Name.

1. Click anywhere in the **Supplier Name** column.

2. Click the **Sort Ascending** button $\begin{smallmatrix}A\\Z\end{smallmatrix}\downarrow$ on the toolbar. Or, if you prefer, select **Records, Sort** and then select **Sort Ascending**. Your table should now look like that in Figure 10.13.

Supplier ID	SupplierName	Address	City	UK
3	Cartiers	Les Halles	Paris	UK
6	Jacksons	Old Yard	Oxford	UK
2	Jacksons	West Gate	Cambridge	UK
5	Scotts	The Green	Manchester	UK
4	Seidels	Das Haus	Cologne	Germany
1	Simpsons	East Gate	Oxford	UK

Figure 10.13 Suppliers table in supplier name order

Now sort the data into descending order of City as follows:

3. Click anywhere in the **City** column.

4. Click the **Sort Descending** button $\begin{smallmatrix}Z\\A\end{smallmatrix}\downarrow$. Your table should now look like that in Figure 10.14.

Finally, return the data to its original order as follows:

5. Click anywhere in the **Supplier ID** field.

6. Click the **Sort Ascending** button.

Q4   *How would you sort the data so that all the UK suppliers were listed first, followed by those in Germany, then France?*

Supplier ID	SupplierName	Address	City	Nation
3	Cartiers	Les Halles	Paris	UK
6	Jacksons	Old Yard	Oxford	UK
1	Simpsons	East Gate	Oxford	UK
5	Scotts	The Green	Manchester	UK
4	Seidels	Das Haus	Cologne	Germany
2	Jacksons	West Gate	Cambridge|	UK

Figure 10.14 Suppliers table in descending order of city

10.8 Filtering a database

Databases are useful not only for sorting data, but also to extract selected information quickly and easily. The Filter command allows you to display a selection of records according to some chosen criteria. You will begin by extracting all the records with the Supplier Name of Jacksons as follows:

1. Move the cursor to the **Supplier Name** field.

2. Select the whole name **Jacksons** either from row 2 or row 6 by positioning the cursor on the name Jacksons and double-clicking on the mouse.

3. Click on the **Filter by Selection** button . Or, if you prefer, select **Records, Filter** then select **Filter by Selection**.

Only the records with supplier name Jacksons will be displayed.

4. Remove the filter you just applied by clicking on the **Remove Filter** button .You will see all the original data in the table again. Or, if you prefer, select **Records, Remove Filter/Sort**.You will see all the original data in the table again.

This time you will extract all the records with City beginning with C as follows:

5. Select the letter **C** from either the city name Cambridge or Cologne.

6. Click on the **Filter by Selection** button.

Only the records with city name beginning with C should appear.

7. Remove the filter again using the **Remove Filter** button.

Q5 *How would you extract all the suppliers with Address ending in d?*

10.9 Closing a database

1. Close the table by clicking the **Close** ☒ button on the Suppliers: Table title bar.

2. Close the database by clicking on the **Close** ☒ button of the Shop: database window. The database will be automatically saved.

3. Close Access by clicking on its **Close** ☒ button.

10.10 Summary

In this chapter you have met the following data definitions:

- The simplest kind of *database* consists of a single table of data.
- Each column in a table is called a *field*.
- Each row in a table is called a *record*.
- The field that identifies each record in a database uniquely is called a *primary key* or *key field*.

10.11 Written exercises

10.11.1 Design a table that might be used by a bank to store information about its customers. The table should include customer details such as name, address and account number. Do not try to include all the information required by a bank: your table should be fairly simple and contain at most ten fields.

10.11.2 Design a simple table that might be used by a school or university to store data about its students. The table should include information such as student name, address and course details. The table should be designed in such a way that it can be sorted in order of examination grades or student surname.

10.11.3 Design a table for storing information about some of the members of your family. The table should be designed in such a way that the family members can be sorted into increasing order of age. It should also be possible to filter the table to extract all the people who bear the same relationship to you, such as sister, cousin or nephew. Add at least six members of your family to the table.

10.12 Practical exercises

10.12.1 Create a new database called **Finances**. This database will be used to store information about your personal finances. Use the Table Wizard to create a table based on the **Expenses** sample table. Add the fields **ExpenseID, AmountSpent, Description, DatePurchased** and **PaymentMethod** to the table. Add the row of data shown in Figure 10.15 to the table. The values in the Amount Spent column can be entered as numbers, but will appear with a currency symbol in front of them. Similarly, the forward slashes (/) in the Date Purchased column are entered automatically: you just type in the day, month and year. The Payment Method can be any kind of text, such as cash or cheque for example.

Expense ID	Amount Spent	Description	Date Purchased	Payment Method
1	£1,500.00	Car	13/12/97	Visa

Figure 10.15 Expenses table

Add at least **five more rows of data** to the table.

10.12.2 Create a new database called **Company**. This database will store information about the employees working in a private company. Then use the **Table Wizard** to create a table based on the **Employees** sample table. Add the following fields to your table: **EmployeeID, SocialSecurityNumber, FirstName, LastName** and **Title**. Enter the data shown in Figure 10.16. The numbers in the Social Security Number field can be typed in without the dashes: these will be inserted automatically.

Perform the following manipulations on the table:

- **Sort** the table into ascending alphabetical order of last name.
- **Filter** the table to extract all records with Title **Dr**.
- **Remove** the filter on the table.
- **Filter** the table to extract all records with First Name beginning with **J**.
- **Remove** the filter on the table.
- **Sort** the table back into its original order.

Employee ID	Social Security Number	First Name	Last Name	Title
1	563-56-1122	Clare	Lewis	Dr
2	221-89-9992	Jane	Smith	Ms
3	553-13-1110	Tom	Jones	Mr
4	441-22-1186	John	Joisce	Dr
5	342-00-7855	Jeremy	Martin	Dr

Figure 10.16 Employees table

10.12.3 Create a new database and give it a name of your choice. Use the **Table Wizard** to add a table to the database, based on any of the sample tables. Add some data to the table and experiment with the **Sort** and **Filter** commands on your new table.

Database Tables

11.1 Overview

In this chapter you will continue to learn more about Access tables. You will begin by examining the table you created in the previous chapter in more detail, so make sure that you have it accessible. In this chapter you will learn how to:

- Open a database.
- Create a table without a wizard.
- Modify a table.
- Edit data in a table.

11.2 Introduction

The structure of a database table should be planned very carefully before the table is implemented on computer. Two important features of a well-designed table have already been discussed in Chapter 10. First, each piece of significant information must be stored in a separate field. Second, each table should usually contain a primary key field. A third design consideration is introduced in this chapter: the choice of data type. All of the tables you have created so far have had data types automatically assigned by the Table Wizard, but in this chapter you will need to assign the data types yourself.

Each field in a database table has a data type associated with it, which corresponds to the kind of values stored in that field. Access has a number of different data types available, some of which are listed in Figure 11.1. If a field has type *Text*, then it can store any text, numbers or other keyboard characters, but its total length must not exceed 255 characters. Sometimes it is useful to store larger amounts of text in a database field. For example, in a database for storing correspondence there might be a field containing the text of each letter. In that case a field of type *Memo* would be appropriate. Like Text fields, Memo fields can also store characters of any kind, but they have a much higher size limit of 64,000 characters. If a field is used to store numerical values, then it should be assigned type *Number*. Numbers can also be stored in Text fields, but it is then difficult to manipulate them or use them in calculations. The *Date/Time* type is used to store dates and times in a variety of formats. *Currency* fields store numbers, but they are displayed together with the appropriate currency symbols, such as pounds or dollars. Fields of type *Auto-Number* are automatically numbered by Access. New records are added to the database either with consecutive or random numbers. These numbers cannot be modified by the user. The *Yes/No* type is used for values that are restricted to two choices such as true or false.

```
Text
Memo
Number
Date/Time
Currency
AutoNumber
Yes/No
```

Figure 11.1 Some Access data types

An example of a table that uses a variety of these data types is given in Figure 11.2. This table shows some of the orders made in a pharmacy over a short period of time.

Order ID	Item	Quantity	UnitPrice	Date	Paid
1	Toothpaste	1000	£1.25	13/12/97	Yes
2	Eye Drops	150	£2.49	18/09/97	No
3	Nasal Spray	300	£2.99	25/10/97	Yes

Figure 11.2 Pharmacy order table

The data type of the first column, Order ID is AutoNumber. This means that each value has a different number: no duplicates are allowed. This is a useful way to ensure that the field is maintained as a primary key field. The second column, Item has type Text, so that anything can be typed into this field. The Quantity column has type Number. This means that if any text other than a number is typed into this field, it will not be accepted. Also, calculations can be performed on numbers elsewhere in the database. The UnitPrice column has type Currency, so the values shown in the column are stored as numbers but displayed as pounds. Date has type Date/Time. This ensures that the data is added into this field in a consistent format. The format in this table is the Short Date form, but it could be set to Long Date for example, in which case the first date would appear in the form 13 December 1997. Paid has type Yes/No. This means that only the words Yes or No can appear in this field, so the user is protected from adding invalid data. All of the fields in Figure 11.2

could have been given type Text, but it would then be more difficult to protect against errors in data entry.

11.3 Opening a database

Databases are opened in Access in exactly the same way that files are opened in Word and Excel. You will now open the database you created in Chapter 10. If your database was stored on floppy disk you will need to insert the disk into the drive before trying to open the database.

1.   If Access is already running, select **File, Open** or click on the **Open** button on the toolbar. Otherwise, start up Access in the same way that you did in the previous chapter. When you see the Access start up screen shown previously in Figure 10.3, click on **OK** to view more files. You will see the Open dialogue box similar to that shown in Figure 11.3.

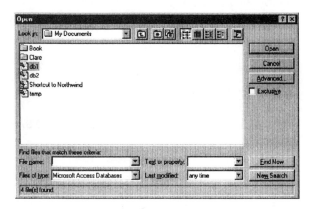

Figure 11.3 Open File dialogue box

2.   Set the **Look in** option to the folder in which you saved the Shop database you created in Chapter 10, by clicking the down arrow on the right of the Look in box and selecting an option. Select the **3½ Floppy (A:)** option if your database is on the floppy disk.

3.   Select the **Shop** database, but do not open it yet.

4.   Click on the **Properties** icon on the toolbar. The full details of the Shop database will appear on the right of the screen, including the Author and the last date it was modified.

Q1   What size is the Shop database?

5.   Click on **Open** to open the database. The screen in Figure 11.4 will appear.

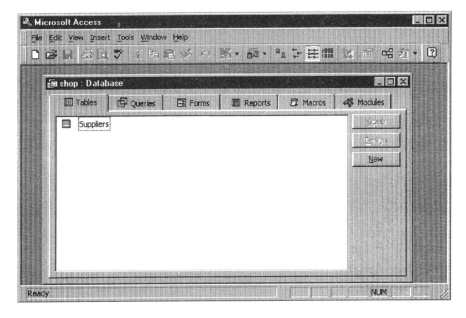

Figure 11.4 Shop database

11.4 Viewing table design

The Shop database contains one table, called Suppliers. There are two different ways of viewing this table: *Datasheet* view and *Design* view. So far, you have only used datasheet view to manipulate tables. Design view is used to see the underlying structure of the table, and to modify it if necessary. You can open a table in either view, and it is then very easy to switch between the two views as you will now see.

1.   Select the **Suppliers** table if it is not already selected, then click on the **Open** button to open the Suppliers table in datasheet view. You will see the six rows of data you entered previously.

2.   Click on the **Table View** icon 📐 to see the table structure, or select **View, Table Design**. You will see the screen in Figure 11.5.

Database tables   135

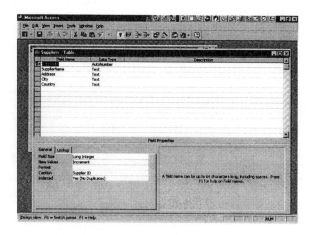

Figure 11.5 Suppliers table in design view

The top half of the screen has three columns: Field Name, Data Type and Description. The Field Name column lists the names of all the fields in the Suppliers table. The Data Type column lists the type of each field. At the moment, all the fields in the table apart from the Suppler ID have type Text. The Description column can contain a description of the contents of each field, but it was left blank by the Table Wizard when this table was created. This description is normally used first by the designer, and later by the end user to see the purpose of each field.

The primary key is indicated in design view by a key symbol next to the field name.

Q2   Which field in the Suppliers table is the primary key?

11.5 Modifying field properties

The bottom half of the Design View screen is headed *Field Properties*. Each field has its own set of properties, and most of them need never be changed, but sometimes it is useful to modify them. In this section you will make some minor modifications to the field properties of the Suppliers table.

1.   Select the **SupplierID** field by clicking the grey square containing the key symbol to the left of the field. The entire row will be highlighted as in Figure 11.6.

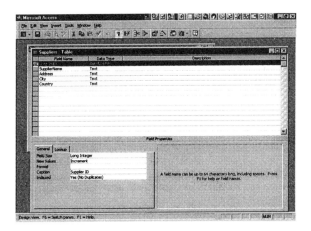

Figure 11.6 Suppliers table with SupplierID field selected

The field properties for the SupplierID field are shown in the bottom half of the screen. The *Caption* property shows which heading is displayed at the top of the SupplierID column when you view the table in datasheet view. The *Indexed* property at the bottom is set to prohibit duplicate entries appearing in this field, which is a necessary restriction for the primary key field. The remaining three properties all control the values that will appear in this field, which in this case are consecutive numbers starting from 1.

Q3   What is the difference between the Caption property and the Field Name value for the SupplierID field?

You will now make some changes to the properties of the Country field.

2.   Select the **Country** field by clicking the grey square to the left of it.

Notice that the list of field properties in the bottom half of the screen changes. This is because the Country field has type Text, unlike the SupplierID field which had type AutoNumber. Each different data type has an associated set of field properties. The properties you will modify for the Country field are the *Field Size, Caption* and *Default Value* properties. The field size shows the maximum size allowed for each value in the Country column. It is currently set to 50. The caption has not yet been set which means that the field name 'Country' is automatically used as a caption until you reset it as you will do below. The default value has not been set, but you will give it the value 'UK'. This means that whenever a new record is added to the table it will automatically have the value 'UK' entered into its Country field. This value can be deleted if the new record is for a foreign supplier.

3.   Change the value of the **Field Size** property to 75.

4.   Type the text **Nation** into the **Caption** property.

5.   Type the text **UK** into the **Default Value** property.

6.   Click the **Table View** icon ▦, or select **View, Datasheet** to see how the caption has changed in the table. You will be asked to save the table before switching views: click **Yes** to do so.

Q4   How has the table changed?

7.   Click the **Table View** icon ◣, or select **View, Design** to return to the table design screen.

8.   Click on **Close** ☒ in the Suppliers: Table window, and save the changes to the design of the Suppliers table.

9.   Click on **Close** ☒ in the Shop: Database window to close the database.

11.6 Creating a table without a wizard

You will now use table design view to create a new table in a new database. All of the tables you have used so far were created with the Access Table Wizard. This is often the quickest way to create a table, but sometimes it is useful to design the whole table from the start since this gives more flexibility. The table you will create will store information about the employees in a small organisation. Follow the steps below to create a new database and then add a new table to it in Design View.

1.   Create a new database by clicking the **New Database** icon, then **OK**. Give it the file name **Staff**, and click on **Create**.

2.   Click the **Tables** tab then click on the **New** button and you will see the New Table dialogue box in Figure 11.7.

3.   Click **Design View** and click **OK** and you will see the empty Table Design screen as shown in Figure 11.8.

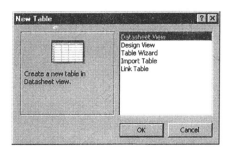

Figure 11.7 New Table dialogue box

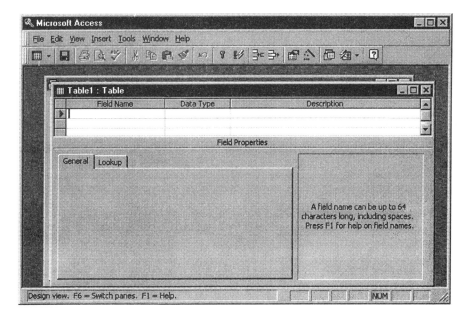

Figure 11.8 Empty Table design view

The table you will create will contain five columns, called IdNo, Name, Date, Salary and Years. The data types and descriptions of the fields are given in Figure 11.9. You will now create a new database to contain this table.

Field Name	Data Type	Description
IdNo	AutoNumber	Staff Identity Number
Name	Text	Employee Name
Date	Date/Time	Date of Arrival
Salary	Currency	Current Annual Salary
Years	Number	Length of Service

Figure 11.9 Data types for the Employees table

4. Type the field name **IdNo** in the first line of the **Field Name** column. Then press **Tab** to move to the next column.

5.	Click on the down arrow 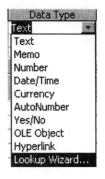 in the **Data Type** column to see the list of available data types, and select **AutoNumber**. Then press **Tab** to move to the next column.

6.	Type the text **Staff Identity Number** in the **Description** column. Then press **Tab** to move to the next line.

7.	Add four more fields to the table, named **Name**, **Date**, **Salary**, and **Years** with data types as shown in the table in Figure 11.9.

The **Years** field is to be used to represent the total number of years worked, and is therefore not necessarily a whole number. The default Field Size property for fields of type Number is *Long Integer*, which means that only whole numbers will be displayed. The Field Size property has to be changed to type *Double* if decimal digits are to be shown. Follow the steps below to change the Years field to the appropriate type.

8.	Select the **Years** field by clicking the grey square to the left of it.

9.	Click in the box marked **Long Integer** in the Field Properties section.

10.	Click on the down arrow that appears on the right of the Long Integer box, and you will see the list of options in Figure 11.10.

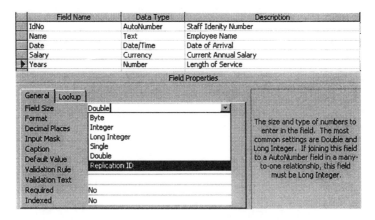

Figure 11.10 Number types

Most of the options in Figure 11.10 are rarely used. The most important ones to remember are Long Integer, for storing whole numbers, and Double, for storing numbers with decimal digits.

11.   Select **Double**.

Carry out the following steps to change the format of the Date field. There are a number of different formats for a field of type Date/Time. In this example you will use the Long Date format.

12.   Select the **Date** field by clicking the grey square to the left of it.

13.   Click in the box marked **Format** in the Field Properties section.

14.   Click on the down arrow that appears on the right of the Long Integer box, and you will see the list of options in Figure 11.11.

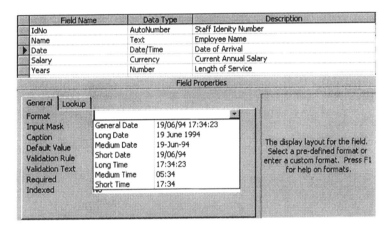

Figure 11.11 Date formats

15.   Select **Long Date**. This means that any values added to the Date field will have to be added in Long Date format.

11.7 Setting the primary key

The last step when creating a table in design view is to allocate a primary key. Follow the steps below to set the primary key in this table to be the IdNo field.

1.   Select the **IdNo** field.

2.   Select **Edit, Primary Key** or click the **Primary key** icon ![key icon] on the toolbar, and a key symbol will appear to the left of the IdNo field name to show that it is now the primary key field (![field IdNo]).

If you make a mistake and put the key symbol next to the wrong field name, you can remove it by selecting **Edit, Undo Primary Key**.

11.8 Saving the table

1.   Switch to **Datasheet View** (![datasheet icon]) to see the table you have created. You will be asked if you want to save your table, so say **Yes**. You will then see the **Save As** dialogue box in Figure 11.12.

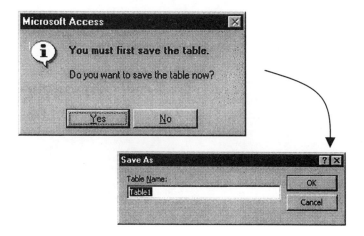

Figure 11.12 Save As dialogue box

2.   Press the **Delete** key to remove the default name, Table1, then type the name **Employees** and click on **OK**. You will see the screen in Figure 11.13.

Q5   What is the difference between datasheet and design view?

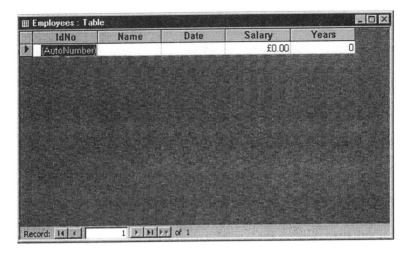

Figure 11.13 Empty Employees table

11.9 Changing table structure

Sometimes you may decide to change the structure of a table after it has been created. Before you add any data to the Employees table, you will try this out by adding a new field to the table, and removing an old one. First, add a new field between the Date and Salary fields by following the instructions below.

1. Switch back to **Design View** (▦).

2. Select the **Salary** field (▶ Salary)

3. Select **Insert, Rows** or click the **Insert Rows** button on the toolbar ᗺᗴ. A new row will appear.

4. Click in the Field Name column of the new row and enter the text **Age**. Then set the Data Type to **Number** and Description to **Employee Age**, as shown in Figure 11.14.

Field Name	Data Type	Description
IdNo	AutoNumber	Staff Idenity Number
Name	Text	Employee Name
Date	Date/Time	Date of Arrival
Age	Number	Employee Age
Salary	Currency	Current Annual Salary
Years	Number	Length of Service

Figure 11.14 Employees table

Now delete the Date field by following the steps below.

5.   Select the **Date** field.

6.   Click on the **Delete Rows** button on the toolbar ⊟→ or press the **Delete** key on the keyboard, and the screen will look like that in Figure 11.15.

Field Name	Data Type	Description
IdNo	AutoNumber	Staff Idenity Number
Name	Text	Employee Name
Age	Number	Employee Age
Salary	Currency	Current Annual Salary
Years	Number	Length of Service

Figure 11.15 Employees table

11.10 Data entry and modification

There are two ways to enter data into a table. One way is to enter it directly in datasheet view as you did in Chapter 10. The other way is to use a *Form*, but you will not learn how to do that until Chapter 13. One advantage of the datasheet method is that it easy to manipulate records when they are all on view in front of you. In this section you will learn how to delete and move records in datasheet view. First you will need to add some data to the table.

1.   Switch back to **Datasheet View** and click **Yes** when asked whether you would like to save the table. Enter the data shown in Figure 11.16. The numbers in the **IdNo** field will be inserted automatically so use **Tab** to move past the IdNo column. The currency symbols in the Salary column will also appear automatically, so you only need to enter the numbers.

IdNo	Name	Age	Salary	Years
1	Yapp	33	£14,000.00	5.2
2	Dodd	41	£13,000.00	8.4
3	Pit	37	£210,000.00	4.7
4	Guy	45	£32,000.00	10.1
5	Brook	52	£35,000.00	9.5
* (AutoNumber)		0	£0.00	0

Figure 11.16 Employees table data

Now that you have created a table of data, you will make some modifications to it. First delete the first record from the table as follows:

2. Select the record with name **Yapp** by clicking on the grey square to the left of it.

3. Press the **Delete** key on the keyboard, or select **Edit, Delete** and you will be asked whether you are sure you want to delete this record. Click on **Yes** to accept the change.

Now move the first record to the bottom of the table by following the steps below.

4. Select the record with name **Dodd**.

5. Click on the **Cut** icon ✂ or select **Edit, Cut**. You will asked whether you are sure you want to delete this item, so click on **Yes**

IdNo	Name	Age	Salary	Years
2	Dodd	41	£13,000.00	8.4
3	Pit	37	£210,000.00	4.7
4	Guy	45	£32,000.00	10.1
5	Brook	52	£35,000.00	9.5

Figure 11.17 Employees table data

6. Select the empty row at the bottom of the table, by clicking on the asterisk (*) symbol to the left of it.

7. Click on the **Paste** icon 📋 or select **Edit, Paste** and the record with name Dodd will appear at the bottom of the table. Its IdNo will have changed to 6.

IdNo	Name	Age	Salary	Years
3	Pit	37	£21,000.00	4.7
4	Guy	45	£32,000.00	10.1
5	Brook	52	£35,000.00	9.5
6	Dodd	41	£13,000.00	8.4
(AutoNumber)		0	£0.00	0

Figure 11.18 Employees table data

Now close the modified table and database in the usual way, as in the steps next.

8. Click on the **Close** ❌ button in the Employees: Table window.

9. Click on the **Close** ❌ button in the Staff: Database window.

11.11 Summary

In this chapter you have met the following database definitions:

- Each field in a table has a *type*.
- Some of the most commonly used types in Access are: Text, Number, Date/Time, Currency, AutoNumber and Yes/No.
- Each table in Access can be viewed in either of two ways: *datasheet* view or *design* view.
- The quickest way to create an Access table is to use the Table Wizard.
- The most flexible way to create an Access table is to use Table Design.

You have also been shown how to do the following:

- Open a database using the **Open** button or the **File, Open** command.
- Create a table in **Table Design view**.
- Modify properies of the data fields in a table.
- Insert and delete rows using the **Insert Rows** and **Delete Rows** buttons and menu commands.
- Edit data in a table using **Edit** commands such as **Cut** and **Paste**.

11.12 Written exercises

11.12.1 Design a table that might be used by a library to maintain a record of all its books. The table should include information about the title, author and subject classification of each book. It should also show whether or not a book is on loan. The data type of each field in the table should be shown clearly on your design. The table must include at least one field of each of the following types: Text, Number, Date/Time, Currency, AutoNumber and Yes/No. Indicate which field is the primary key. The layout of your table design should be similar to Figure 11.9.

11.12.2 Design a table to hold information about all the courses you are currently taking. The table should use a variety of different Access data types. Add at least five rows of sample data to the table.

11.12.3 Design a table that might be used by a sports centre to hold booking information about its various facilities. These might include squash and tennis courts, saunas, jacuzzis and a multigym for example. The table should show how much each facility costs to hire, and give the date and time of each booking. Use appropriate data types for each of the fields in the table, and add at least six rows of data to it. The table should be designed in such a way that it is possible to extract all the bookings on any given day and sort them into increasing order of time.

11.13 Practical exercises

11.13.1 In this exercise you will create and modify a database which stores a list of all the forthcoming events at a small arts centre.

a) Create a new database called **Arts**.

b) Create a table with the structure shown in Figure 11.19.

Field Name	Data Type
EventID	AutoNumber
Title	Text
Type	Text
Time	Date/Time
Date	Date/Time
Price	Currency

Figure 11.19 Arts centre data types

c) Set the primary key to be **EventID**.

d) One of the properties of the **Title** field is called **Required**. This property shows whether a value must always be added to this column in a table, or whether it can be left blank. The Title column entry must never be left blank, so change this property from No to **Yes**.

e) Change the **Format** property of the **Time** field to **Short Time**.

f) Change the **Format** property of the **Date** field to **Medium Date**.

g) Insert a new field in between the Date and Price fields, with field name **TicketsSold** and data type **Number**.

h) Add the data shown in Figure 11.20 to the table.

i) Sort the table into increasing order of price.

EventID	Title	Type	Time	Date	TicketsSold	Price
1	Les Miserables	Theatre	20:00	01-May-97	145	£8.50
2	Shine	Film	19:30	02-May-97	190	£3.50
3	Kimbara	Jazz	20:00	04-May-97	97	£5.00
4	Matilda	Film	14:30	06-May-97	156	£3.50
5	The Wolves	Theatre	20:00	07-May-97	200	£9.50

Figure 11.20 Arts centre data

11.13.2 Create a new database called **Music**. Design and implement a table to list all the items in your personal music collection. The table should be designed in such a way that it can be filtered to extract a list of all CDs, records or cassettes. Include at least five fields and ten rows of data in the table. The field names you choose must not use any of the following five characters: . ! ` [ ]

11.13.3 Create a table in a new database which could be used by a television broadcasting company to store the forthcoming schedule of programmes. The table should include the date and time of transmission for each programme. There should also be a field of type Yes/No to indicate whether subtitles are available or not. Add at least six fields and five rows of data to the table.

12 Relationships

12.1 Overview

In this chapter you will learn how to create databases containing more than one table. Specifically, you will learn how to:

- Create multiple tables.
- Create relationships between tables.
- View relationships.
- Edit relationships.

12.2 Introduction

All of the databases you have created so far have consisted of a single table of data. In principle, every database can be stored as one table, but in practice this can cause a number of problems. For example, consider the table of sausage products in Figure 12.1. Each sausage variety is listed together with the supplier name and address, price per kilo and availability information.

ProductID	Supplier Name	Address	City	Nation	Description	UnitPrice	Discontinued
B1	Simpsons	East Gate	Oxford	UK	Beef	£1.20	☐
C1	Scotts	The Green	Manchester	UK	Cocktail	£1.80	☑
C2	Cartiers	Les Halles	Paris	France	Chorizo	£2.75	☐
C3	Scotts	The Green	Manchester	UK	Cumberland	£1.25	☐
G1	Simpsons	East Gate	Oxford	UK	Garlic	£2.50	☐
L1	Jacksons	Old Yard	Oxford	UK	Lamb	£1.60	☑
P1	Jacksons	West End	Cambridge	UK	Pork	£1.50	☐
V1	Scotts	The Green	Manchester	UK	Venison	£1.75	☐
W1	Seidels	Das Haus	Cologne	Germany	Wurst	£3.45	☑

Figure 12.1 Products table

149

There are two problems with this table. First, it contains a lot of duplication. For example, there are three products from the supplier named Scotts, and the full supplier address has been included in the record of each. So if the supplier were to change address it would not be very easy to update the database: the address in every duplicate row would have to be changed consistently. The second problem with this table is one of information loss. For example, there is only one product from the supplier called Seidels, so if this product were deleted from the table, the name and address of the supplier would be lost. Clearly, it would be more sensible to separate the supplier records from the product records. A much better design for this database is given by the two tables in Figure 12.2. This shows the familiar Suppliers table created in Chapter 10, together with a separate table of products. The two tables are related to each other by the SupplierID field, which shows which supplier is associated with each product.

ProductID	SupplierID	Description	UnitPrice	Discontinued
B1	1	Beef	£1.20	☐
C1	5	Cocktail	£1.80	☑
C2	3	Chorizo	£2.75	☐
C3	5	Cumberland	£1.25	☐
G1	1	Garlic	£2.50	☐
L1	6	Lamb	£1.60	☑
P1	2	Pork	£1.75	☐
V1	5	Venison	£1.75	☐
W1	4	Wurst	£3.45	☑

Supplier ID	SupplierName	Address	City	UK
1	Simpsons	East Gate	Oxford	UK
2	Jacksons	West Gate	Cambridge	UK
3	Cartiers	Les Halles	Paris	UK
4	Seidels	Das Haus	Cologne	Germany
5	Scotts	The Green	Manchester	UK
6	Jacksons	Old Yard	Oxford	UK

Figure 12.2 Separated Products and Suppliers tables

Unlike the original Products table in Figure 12.1, the new table in Figure 12.2 no longer contains the duplicated supplier names and addresses. Instead, only the SupplierID is repeated on different products from the same supplier. The problem of information loss has also been removed, since the product from supplier Seidels can now be deleted from the Products table without losing the supplier name and address in the Suppliers table.

The name given to this process of dividing up data into separate, related tables is *normalisation*. The name given to the resulting database containing one or more tables is a *relational* database.

The most common type of relationship between any two tables in a relational database is called a *one-to-many* relationship. This means that a record in the first table can be related to several in the second, but each record in the second table is only related to one in the first. For example, the relationship between the Suppliers and Products tables in Figure 12.2 is one-to-many because each supplier can be related to several products. For example, Scotts is related to three products, and Simpsons is related to two. Conversely, each product is only related to one supplier only: the one that is referred to in the SupplierID field of the order.

There are two other kinds of relationship that can exist between database tables: *one-to-one* relationships and *many-to-many* relationships. In a one-to-one relationship, each record in one table is related to at most one record in the other table. So the relationship between the Suppliers and Products tables would be one-to-one if each supplier were only allowed to supply one product. One-to-one relationships are not common because tables which are related in this way are usually combined into one. If each supplier were only related to one product, then the problem of duplication in Figure 12.1 would be removed, so the need to separate the table into two would not be so great. The last kind of relationship is many-to-many. In this kind of relationship each record in either table can be related to several in the other. Most of the exercises in this chapter will focus on one-to-many relations, since many-to-many relationships can only be created in Access by using two one-to-many relationships. Some examples of many-to-many relationships are given in the exercises at the end of the chapter.

12.3 Creating a new table

Before you can create any relationships in your Shop database, you will need to create another table. You will begin by creating the Products table in Figure 12.2, and then you will create the one-to-many relationship between the Suppliers and Products tables. Make sure that the Shop database is accessible, then follow the steps below to create the new table.

1.   Start up Access and open the **Shop** database.

2.   Create a new table in Design View with the structure shown in Figure 12.3.

Field Name	Data Type	Description
▶ ProductID	Text	Product number
SupplierID	Number	Supplier identity number
Description	Text	Description of sausage
UnitPrice	Currency	Price per kilo
Discontinued	Yes/No	Current product availability

Figure 12.3 Products table structure

Q1   *What was the type of the SupplierID field in the Suppliers table?*

The reason for the difference is that the numbers in the SupplierID field of the Products table are not entered automatically, since they refer to numbers in the Suppliers table.

3.   Set the primary key to be **ProductID**.

4.   **Close** ✖ the table and save it to the name **Products**.

You will not add the data to the table until you have created the relationship between the Suppliers and Products tables. It is important to create the relationship before adding data, because then Access can ensure that you do not make mistakes when filling in the SupplierID column of the Products table.

12.4 Building a relationship

You have now created two tables to contain information about products. One table, Products, will list all the outstanding products, and the other one, Suppliers, lists the names and addresses of each of the suppliers. The two tables have a common field: SupplierID. It is now time to use that field to link them together by following the steps below.

1.   Select **Tools**, **Relationships** or click on the **Relationships** icon 🖧. You will see the Show Table dialogue box in Figure 12.4.

2.   Click on **Suppliers**, then click on the **Add** button to add it to the relationship. The list of fields in the Suppliers table will appear in the Relationships window, but it may be obscured by the Show Table window. You can move the Show Table window by dragging its blue title line.

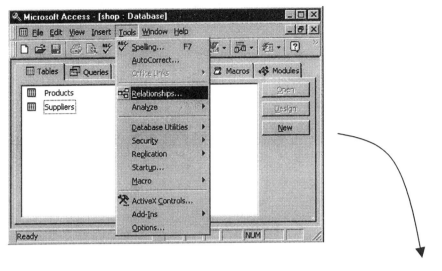

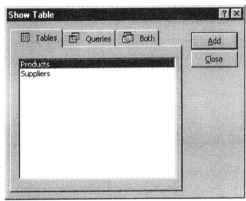

Figure 12.4 Show Table dialogue box

3.   Click on **Products**, then click on **Add** again.

4.   Click on the **Close** ✖ button in the **Show Table** window. You will see the Relationships window in Figure 12.5.

5.   Click on the **SupplierID** field in the **Suppliers** table.

6.   Press down on the left mouse button and drag the pointer towards the **Products** table. The appearance of the pointer will change while you are dragging it. It will appear first as a small rectangle then as a circle. Move the pointer on top of the word **SupplierID** in the **Products** table, then release it. You will see the Relationships dialogue box in Figure 12.6.

Relationships   153

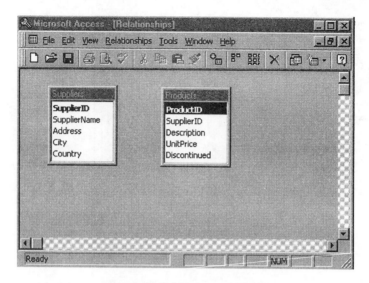

Figure 12.5 Relationships window

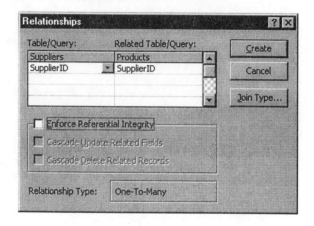

Figure 12.6 Relationships dialogue box

Notice that the Relationship Type shown at the bottom of the window is set to One-To-Many, because each supplier can be related to many products. Access has automatically selected this type of relationship because the SupplierID is the primary key in the Suppliers table, but not in the Products table. So each record in the Suppliers table could be related to several in the Products table, since the SupplierID field in the Products table can contain duplicates. But conversely, each record in the Products table cannot be related to more than one in the Suppliers table.

Before you finish creating the relationship between the two tables, you must choose a *Referential Integrity* option. Referential Integrity options prevent you from making mistakes when you are adding data to the tables in your database. If you do not enforce referential integrity then it is possible to add an order to the Products table for which there is no corresponding supplier.

7. Click on the check box to the left of **Enforce Referential Integrity** option. The two greyed out options below will change to black:

    - **Cascade Update Related Fields** If you select this option and you make a change to a SupplierID value in the Suppliers table, then the corresponding SupplierID in the Products table will be automatically changed too.
    - **Cascade Delete Related Fields** If you select this option and then delete a supplier, say Simpsons, from the Suppliers table, then all the products supplied by Simpsons will automatically be deleted from the Products table.

Q2   Which products would disappear from the Products table if you had selected the Cascade Delete Related Fields option and then deleted the supplier named Scotts from the Suppliers table?

8. Select neither of the above options, then Access will issue an error message if you try to add fields to the Products table that do not match an entry in the Suppliers table. Then click on the **Create** button. You will see the Relationships window in Figure 12.7.

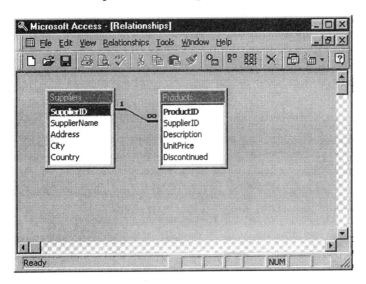

Figure 12.7 Relationships window

The line between the two tables shows that they are related. The **1** symbol next to the Suppliers table, and many (∞) symbol next to the Products table shows that one supplier can be connected to many products.

9. Click on the **Close** ☒ button in the Relationships window and you will be asked whether you want to save the changes to the layout of relationships. Click on **Yes**.

Now that the relationship has been created you can add the product data to the table.

10. **Open** the **Products** table and enter the data shown in Figure 12.2 at the start of the chapter. Each type of sausage is listed together with its price per kilo and availability information.

11. **Close** ☒ the Products table again.

Q3 *What would happen if you had entered the ProductID C2 for Cumberland sausages instead of C3?*

12.5 Extending a relationship

In this section you will add a third table to the Shop database, and modify the relationships accordingly. The third table is called Orders and contains a list of orders made by the shop to its suppliers. Each product must be ordered separately, so each order refers to only one product, but the same product may be ordered several times. Therefore the relationship between the Products and Orders table will be one-to-many again. Follow the steps below to create the Orders table.

1. Create a new table in Design view with the structure shown in Figure 12.8.

Q4 *Why is the data type of the SupplierID field not set to AutoNumber as it is in the Suppliers table?*

Field Name	Data Type	Description
OrderID	Text	Order number
Date	Date/Time	Date of issue
ProductID	Text	Product identity number
Quantity	Number	Number of kilos ordered

Figure 12.8 Structure of the Orders table

2. Set the primary key to be **OrderID**.

3. Select the **Date** field, and change its **Format** property to **Medium Date**.

4. Click on **Close** ![X] and save the table to the name **Orders**.

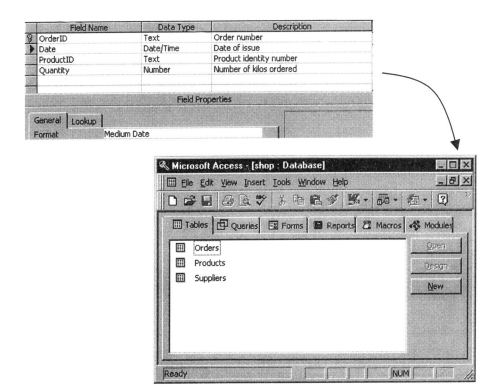

Figure 12.9 Resulting table

Now create the relationship between the Products and Orders tables by following the steps below.

5. Click on the **Relationships** icon or select **Tools, Relationships**.

6. Click on the **Show Table** icon ![icon], or select **Relationships, Show Table**. You will see the same Show Table dialogue box that appeared previously in Figure 12.4. The Orders table is now listed together with the Products and Suppliers tables.

7. Click on **Orders**, then click **Add**.

8.   Click on the **Close** ☒ button in the Show Table window. You will see
      the screen in Figure 12.10.

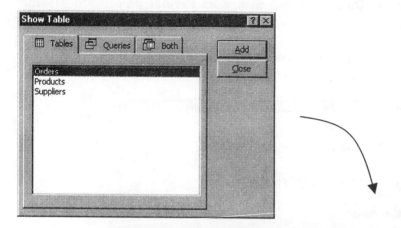

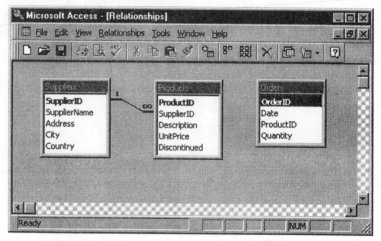

Figure 12.10 Relationships window

9.   Create a one-to-many link between **ProductID** fields in the **Products**
      and **Orders** tables in the same way that you created the link between
      Suppliers and Products before. Remember to tick the box marked **En-
      force Referential Integrity** before you create the relationship. The re-
      lationship window should now look like that shown in Figure 12.11.

Q5   *What would happen if you forgot to enforce referential integrity and
      then added an order to the Orders table with ProductID J3?*

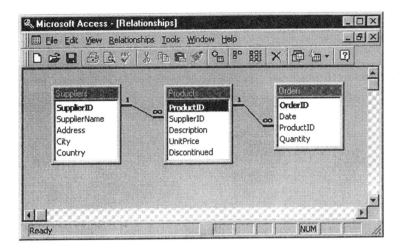

Figure 12.11 Relationships window

12.6 Deleting a relationship

You will delete a relationship and then add it back to the database in order to practise deletion.

1. Select the relationship you just created by moving the mouse pointer onto the line that joins the Products and Orders tables and clicking it. The line will appear slightly more emboldened. Then press the **Delete** key. The message box in Figure 12.12 will appear.

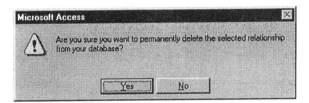

Figure 12.12 Deletion message box

2. Click **Yes** to delete the relationship, and it will disappear.

3. Now add the link between Products and Orders again using the **ProductID** field again as you did in Section 12.5. Remember to enforce referential integrity.

12.7 Viewing a relationship

Sometimes you may wish to change the properties of a relationship after it has been created. For example, you may make a mistake in the original relationship and connect the wrong fields, or you may forget to enforce referential integrity. The technique for viewing and editing a relationship is not obvious. You will try it out now by viewing the relationship between the Products and Suppliers tables, but you will not make any changes.

1. Double click on the line connecting the **Suppliers** and **Products** tables. You will see the Relationships window in which you originally created the relationship as in Figure 12.6.

2. Do not make any changes to the relationship for now. Just click on **Close** ✕ to close the window.

3. Click on **Close** ✕ in the main Relationships window as well, and you will be asked if you want to change the layout of the relationships, so click on **Yes**.

OrderID	Date	ProductID	Quantity
SM123	11-Jun-97	B1	45
JO554	13-Aug-97	G1	100
SM124	20-May-97	V1	120
SC089	27-Jan-97	P1	30
CP089	15-Nov-96	C2	50
SO331	30-Apr-97	B1	60
SM125	23-Sep-97	P1	35
SO332	10-Feb-97	C3	80
SM126	14-Dec-96	C2	100
JC045	02-Feb-97	P1	90
			0

Figure 12.13 Orders table data

4. Now that the relationships have been completed, you can add the data shown in Figure 12.13 to the Orders table.

5. Click on **Close** ✕ in the Orders table, and then **Close** ✕ the Shop: database.

12.8 Summary

In this chapter you have met the following database definitions:

- *Normalisation* is the name given to the process of organising data into a collection of well-structured tables, so that problems like the unnecessary repetition of data are minimised.
- A *relational database* consists of a number of tables that are related together in some way
- A *one-to-many* relationship is one where one record in one table is related to several in another, but each record in the second table is only related to one in the first.
- A *one-to-one* relationship is one where each record in one table is related to at most one record in the other table.
- A *many-to-many* relationship is one where each record in either table can be related to several in the other. In Access this must be created using two one-to-many relationships.
- *Referential integrity* is a constraint that ensures that records in one table are matched correctly with those in another.

You have also been shown how to do the following:

- Create relationships using the **Relationships** icon, or the **Tools, Relationships** command.
- Extend relationships using **Relationships, Show Table**.
- View, edit and delete relationships by clicking on them in the Relationships window.

12.9 Written exercises

12.9.1   Design two tables that could be used together to store information about the courses at a college of higher education. One table should list all the courses, and the other should list the lecturers. Include the data types of each field in your design, and add some sample data to the tables. Assuming that each lecturer may teach several courses, what kind of relationship exists between the two tables?

12.9.2   Design two tables for storing information about your family. One table should hold the personal details about each member of the family, and the other table should store their addresses. State what kind of relationship exists between the two tables.

12.9.3 Design two tables to store data about a subject of your choice. Design the tables so that there is a one-to-many relationship between them, and include some sample data in your design.

12.9.4 Design three tables that could be used by a police station to store information about criminal suspects. One table should contain a list of crimes currently being investigated, and have primary key **CrimeID**. Another table should hold a list of all known criminals, and have primary key **CriminalID**. The third table should have just two fields: CrimeID and CriminalID, and should relate all the crimes to the criminals who are suspected of committing them. Assuming that each crime may have many suspects, and each criminal may be suspected of many crimes, state how the tables are related to each other.

12.10 Practical exercises

12.10.1 Create a new database called **Cars**. Add two tables to the database. The first one, called **Makers**, should contain information about car manufacturers. The second one, called **Models**, should contain information about different kinds of car. One of the fields in the Models table should have the same name as the primary key in the Makers table, to indicate which company manufactures each type of car. Use this field to create a relationship between the tables.

12.10.2 Create a new database called **Football**. Add two tables to the database: one called **Teams** and another called **Players**. The Players table should include a field to indicate which team each player belongs to. No player can belong to more than one team. Create an appropriate relationship between the tables.

12.10.3 Create a new database called **CDs** to store detailed information about a CD collection. Add three tables to the database. The first table, called **Companies** should contain a list of all record companies. The second table, called **Artists** should contain a list of all recording artists. Each entry in the Artists table is either a band or a solo artist. The Artists table should include a field to indicate which record company each band or artist is signed to. No artist can record with more than one company. The third table, called **Albums** should contain a list of all the CDs in the collection. It should include a field to indicate which artist made the album. You can assume that each album was made by a single band or artist: none of the albums are compilations. Create suitable relationships between the Companies and Artists tables, and between the Artists and CDs tables.

12.10.4 Create a new database called **Library**. Add three tables to store information about books on loan. One table should contain a list of books in the library, and have primary key **BookID**. Another table should hold a list of members of the library, and have primary key **CustomerID**. The third table should have two fields: BookID and CustomerID, and should relate all the books on loan to the people who have borrowed them. This table does not have a primary key. Each person can take several books out of the library at a time, and there are many copies of each book, so each one may be taken out by several different people at the same time. Create appropriate relationships between the tables. What kind of relationship is there between the table of books and the table of library members?

13 Queries

Queries

13.1 Overview

A *query* is a technique for sorting and filtering data that is more flexible than the ones you have used before. In this chapter you will learn how to create queries in Access. You will cover the following topics:

* Creating a query with the Query Wizard.
* Viewing query design.
* Modifying a query.
* Adding calculations to a query.

13.2 Introduction

A query can be thought of as a question to the database. For example, a question to the Shop database might be: which suppliers are based in the UK? This is a particularly simple question that could be answered by using a simple filter of the kind you met in Chapter 10. A filter on the Suppliers table to extract all the suppliers with the value 'UK' in the Country field would answer this question. A more difficult question to answer using a filter would be: which products come from UK suppliers? The problem with this question is that the list of supplier addresses is stored in a different table from the list of products. The only reference to suppliers in the Products table of the Shop database is to the Supplier ID, so it would not be easy to filter the Products table to extract all the products from UK suppliers. Instead, a query could be used to extract data from both the Suppliers and Products tables at the same time.

Queries do not necessarily draw data together from separate tables. A query can be based on a single table, like an ordinary sort or filter. Queries that do combine tables do not have to use all the fields from all the tables they combine. For example, the query that extracts all the products from UK suppliers might just extract the Country field of the Suppliers table with some of the fields from the Products table. The Country field will not necessarily be displayed. In this chapter you will construct a query that extracts data from the

Suppliers and Products tables to produce a list of the same information as that held in the original products table of Figure 12.1 in Chapter 12. You will then filter this table to extract a variety of different kinds of information. You will also learn how to use a query to perform calculations.

13.3 Creating a query

You will now create the simple query that extracts data from the Suppliers and Products tables in the Shop database. The quickest way to create a query is to use the Query Wizard. Follow the steps below to create the query.

1.   Start up Access and open the **Shop** database.

2.   Click the **Queries** tab, then click on the **New** button and you will see the New Query dialogue box in Figure 13.1.

3.   Click **Simple Query Wizard** and click OK.

You will see the Simple Query Wizard dialogue box in Figure 13.2. This dialogue box allows you to select fields from any of the tables or queries already in your database and add them to your query.
    In order to extract the data shown in Figure 12.1, you must add each of the fields in the table to the query. Access will then use the relationship that was set up between the Products and Suppliers tables to perform the extraction. This relationship was based on the SupplierID field, but this field is not shown in Figure 12.1, so you will need to add all the fields from the Suppliers and Products tables, apart from the SupplierID field. First you will add the required fields from the Products table. Fields are added to a query in the Query Wizard in the same way that they are added to a table in the Table Wizard.

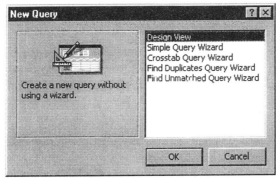

Figure 13.1 New Query dialogue box

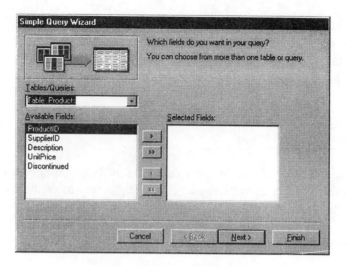

Figure 13.2 Simple Query Wizard

4. Select **Table: Products** from the **Tables/Queries** drop-down box if it is not already selected.

5. Click on the **ProductID** field in the **Available Fields** list, if it is not already highlighted. Then click on the ⟩ button to move it to the **Selected Fields** list.

6. Add the **Description**, **UnitPrice** and **Discontinued** fields to the **Selected Fields** list in the same way so that the screen looks like that in Figure 13.3. If you make a mistake, you can use the ⟨ button to remove a field from the Selected Fields list.

Now you will add the required fields from the Suppliers table. This time you will add the fields in a slightly different way, which can be quicker if you have a large number of fields to add to a query or table. The fields from the Suppliers table should be added in between the ProductID and Date fields since this is where they appear in the original Products table.

7. Click the **ProductID** field in the **Selected Fields** column to select the position in which the new fields will be added to the list.

8. Select **Table: Suppliers** from the **Tables/Queries** drop-down box.

9. Click the ⟩⟩ button to add all the fields in the **Available Fields** column to the **Selected Fields** column. The fields will be inserted into the list between the ProductID and Date fields.

166 *Mastering Microsoft Office*

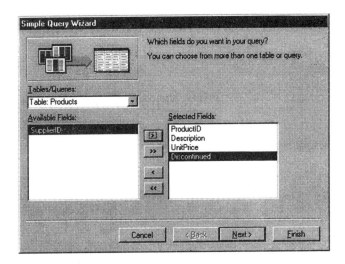

Figure 13.3 Simple Query Wizard

10. Click on the **SupplierID** field, then click on the ◄ button to move the SupplierID field back into the Available Fields list, since the original table in Figure 12.1 does not contain this field (see Figure 13.4).

11. Click **Next** and you will see a box which asks whether you would like a detail or summary query. A detail query displays the selected fields for all the extracted records, and a summary query will produce one line of details, containing the result of a simple calculation such as Average or Sum, on a field in all the extracted records.

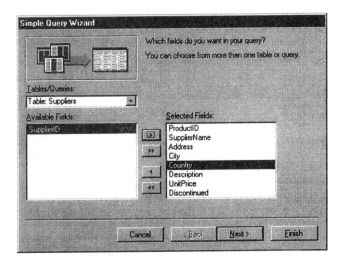

Figure 13.4 Simple Query Wizard

12. Click **Next** again to accept the default option of a detail query. The dialogue box in Figure 13.5 appears so that you can enter a title for the query.

13. Type the title **SortedProducts** into the box headed **What title do you want for your query?** and click **Finish**. The screen shown in Figure 13.6 will appear. The products are not sorted at this stage, but you will add the sorting criteria later in Section 13.5.

The SortedProducts query shows the same data as the original table of Figure 12.1, but in a slightly different order. The problems associated with the orginal table do not apply to the SortedProducts query. For example, if the supplier named Scotts were to change address it would not be necessary to alter the address in each of the rows where Scotts appears in the SortedProducts query. Instead, the change of address could be made once, in the Suppliers table, and each row of the query would change automatically.

Also, if the product from supplier Seidels were deleted from the Products table, it would no longer appear in the SortedProducts query, but the supplier address would still be retained in the Suppliers table.

Q1   *What would happen to the SortedProducts query if the name Simpsons was changed to Wilsons in the Suppliers table?*

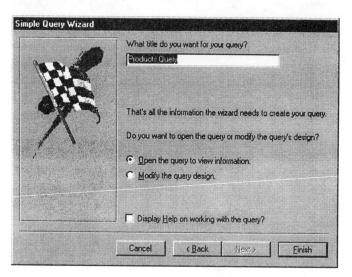

Figure 13.5 Title dialogue box

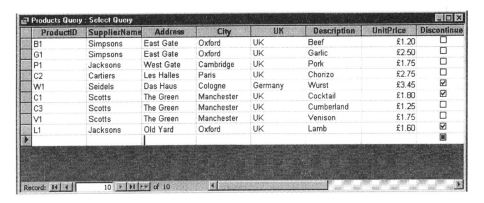

Figure 13.6 SortedProducts query

13.4 Viewing query design

Queries, like tables, can be examined either in datasheet view or design view. There is also a third way to view a query called *SQL*, which is short for *structured query language*, but this topic will not be covered in this book. The method for switching between datasheet and design view for queries is exactly the same as it is for tables, as you will now see.

1. Click on the **Query View** icon to see the query design. You will see the screen in Figure 13.7.

The top half of the screen shows the two tables that were used to construct the query: Suppliers and Products. The line joining the tables shows the SupplierID relationship between them. The bottom half of the screen shows all the fields that were added to the query. Not all of the fields can fit on the screen, so you need to scroll right to see them all.

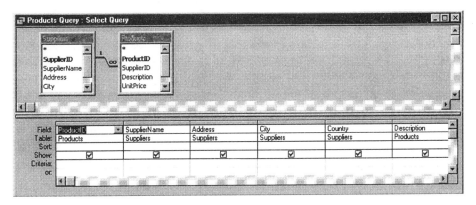

Figure 13.7 SortedProducts query design

The first row in the bottom half of the screen has the title *Field*. This row lists the field names in the query. The next row, *Table* shows which table each field comes from. The rows titled *Sort, Criteria* and *or* will be discussed in Sections 13.5 and 13.6. The row called *Show* is used to control which fields are displayed when the query is viewed in datasheet view. At the moment all the fields are ticked, so they will all be displayed. If you do not want a field to be displayed then you can click on the tick in its Show row to make it disappear.

13.5 Sorting a query

The data in a query can be sorted by any field name, just as the data in an ordinary table can. You will now sort the data into ascending order of Supplier-Name.

1. Click on the **Sort** row of the **SupplierName** column. A small down-arrow will appear to show that a drop-down list is available. Click on the arrow and select **Ascending** from the list of available options (see Figure 13.8).

2. Click on the **Run** icon ❗ to see the result of the query. The records will be sorted into alphabetical order of Supplier name as in Figure 13.9.

3. Click on **Close** ☒ in the **SortedProducts: SelectQuery** window, and you will be asked whether you want to save the query. Click on **Yes** to save it and return to the Shop: Database main window.

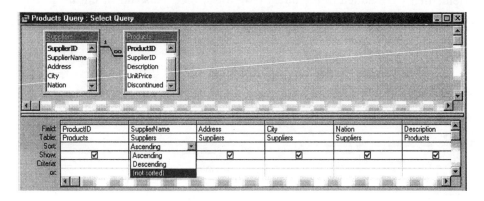

Figure 13.8 Select query

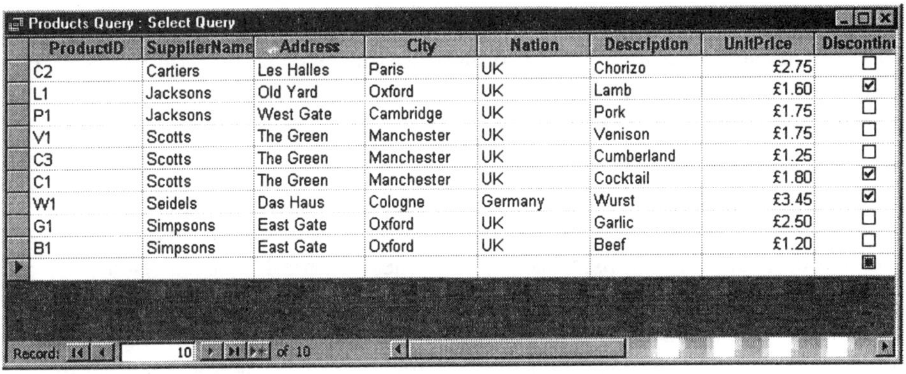

Products Query : Select Query

ProductID	SupplierName	Address	City	Nation	Description	UnitPrice	Discontin
C2	Cartiers	Les Halles	Paris	UK	Chorizo	£2.75	☐
L1	Jacksons	Old Yard	Oxford	UK	Lamb	£1.60	☑
P1	Jacksons	West Gate	Cambridge	UK	Pork	£1.75	☐
V1	Scotts	The Green	Manchester	UK	Venison	£1.75	☐
C3	Scotts	The Green	Manchester	UK	Cumberland	£1.25	☐
C1	Scotts	The Green	Manchester	UK	Cocktail	£1.80	☑
W1	Seidels	Das Haus	Cologne	Germany	Wurst	£3.45	☑
G1	Simpsons	East Gate	Oxford	UK	Garlic	£2.50	☐
B1	Simpsons	East Gate	Oxford	UK	Beef	£1.20	☐

Record: 10 of 10

Figure 13.9 SortedProducts query in Supplier Name order

The SortedProducts query is now part of the Shop database structure, like the tables and relationships you have created before. If you open it again now, you will see the same table of data as in Figure 13.9. If you open it at some future time, when more data has been added to the Suppliers and Products tables, it will show a new list of all the products in the database sorted by Supplier Name. One of the important differences between a query and an ordinary sort or filter applied directly to a table is that the design of a sort or filter cannot be saved for future use, but a query can. A typical database will contain several queries for extracting various kinds of useful information. The criteria used to extract the information in a query need not be restricted to a simple sort or filter. You will start to experiment with some criteria for creating filters in Section 13.6.

13.6 Adding criteria to a query

The data in a query is filtered by entering an expression into the Criteria row of one or more fields in Query Design view. Some of the standard operators that can be used in expressions are listed in Figure 13.10.

<	Less than
<=	Less than or equal
>	Greater than
>=	Greater than or equal
=	Equal
<>	Not equal

Figure 13.10 Comparison operators

So for example, the expression that would be added to Criteria row of the UnitPrice field to extract all the products costing over £2.00 would be >2. The comparison operators in Figure 13.10 are not only used on numbers: they can also be used on dates and ordinary text. So if the expression < > Jacksons were added to the Criteria row of the Supplier Name column, only those records with supplier name other than Jacksons would appear.

Some other familiar operators that can be used in criteria expressions are the wildcard characters: asterisk (*) and question mark (?). As usual, the asterisk can represent any string of characters and the question mark can represent any single character. So the expression S* represents any word beginning with S whereas the expression S?t represents any three letter word beginning with S and ending with t.

You will now experiment with the effects of various kinds of criteria. Normally, you would create a new query, then add some criteria to it, run it and save it for future use. But the easiest way to practise using a number of different criteria will be to make some modifications to the SortedProducts query you have already created and try them out. You will not save any of the changes at the end. You will start by removing the sort criteria and adding some new criteria to extract all the records with city name beginning with C.

1. Select the **SortedProducts** query and click on **Design** to open it up in Design View.

2. Delete the word **Ascending** from the SupplierName column.

3. Type the text **C*** into the **Criteria** row of the **City** column. If you press Enter when you finish typing the criteria, it will change to *Like "C*"*, but this has the same meaning.

4. Click on the **Run** icon to see the result of the query, or alternatively click on the Query View icon which has the same effect. Only the records with City name beginning with C will appear as shown in Figure 13.11.

Q2   *How would you extract all the products from suppliers with name beginning with S?*

You will now remove the criteria you just added to the City field, and add some new criteria. This time you will extract all records with the UnitPrice less than £2.00.

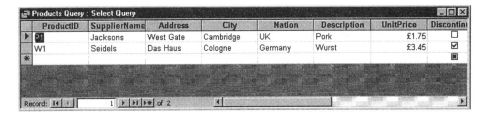

Figure 13.11 Query result

5. Click on the **Query View** icon again, and delete the text **Like "C*"** from the SupplierName column.

6. Scroll along to the **UnitPrice** column, and type the expression **<2** into its **Criteria** row.

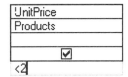

7. Click on **Run** to see the result of the query. Only the records with values below £2.00 in the UnitPrice column will appear, as shown in Figure 13.12.

You will now extract all the products made by non-British suppliers.

8. Click on the **Query View** icon and delete the expression **<2** from the **UnitPrice** column

9. Type the text **<>UK** into the **Criteria** row of the **Country** column. If you press Enter the text will change to **<>"UK"** but it has the same meaning.

Figure 13.12 Query result

Q3   How would you extract all products costing over £1.50?

10.   Click on **Run** to see the result of the query. Only the products made in France and Germany will appear.

11.   Switch back to query design view and delete the text from Criteria row of the **Country** column.

Q4   How would you extract all the products from suppliers who are not based in the city of Manchester?

13.7 Combining criteria

All the queries you have created so far have only contained criteria in one column at a time. But expressions can be added to as many columns as you like. If you enter expressions into the Criteria row of a number of columns, then the data will be filtered to extract only the records which satisfy all the criteria. You will now try this out by extracting all the products from UK suppliers apart from the supplier named Simpsons.

1.   Type the text **UK** into the **Criteria** row of the **Country** column.

2.   Add the text **<>Simpsons** to **Criteria** row of the **SupplierName** column.

3.   Click on **Run** to see the result of the query. Only the records with Country value UK and supplier names other than Simpsons will appear.

Sometimes you might wish to extract all the records which satisfy either one of two criteria, but not necessarily both. In that case you must enter the first expression into the Criteria row and the second one into the *or:* row. Try this out now by following the steps to extract all the products that were either made in France or Oxford.

4.   Switch back to query design view and delete the criteria from the **Country** and **SupplierName** columns.

5.   Type the text **France** into the **Criteria** row of the **Country** column.

6.   Type the text **Oxford** into the **or** row of the **City** column.

7. Click on **Run** to see the result of the query. Only the records with City name Oxford or Nation France will appear.

Q5   How would you extract a list of products which either cost less than £2.00, or are made by Cartiers?

You can add as many expressions as you like to Criteria and or: rows of a query: you are not restricted to just two. A problem may still arise if you want to filter for two expressions on the same field though. For example, you may wish to extract all the products that are over £1.00 and under £2.00. In that case you need to use the *And* keyword. Try this out in the steps below.

8. Go back to **Query Design** view and delete the criteria in the **City** and **Country** columns.

9. Add the text **>1 And <2** to the **Criteria** row of the **UnitPrice** column.

10. Click on **Run** to see the result of the query. Only the records with values in the Amount column that are between £1.00 and £2.00 and will appear.

11. Click on **Close** ☒ in the **SortedProducts: Select Query** window to close the query, and you will be asked whether you would like to save the changes. Click on **No** to leave the query as it was before you began to experiment with the criteria.

| 13.8 Creating a query without a wizard |

You will now use query design view to create a new query in the Shop database. This time it will be based on the Orders and Products tables.

1. Click the **Queries** tab if it is not current, then click on the **New** button and you will see the New Query dialogue box of Figure 13.1 again.

2. Click **Design View** and click **OK** and the **Show Table** dialogue box in Figure 13.13 will appear.

The Show Table box is the same as the one you used in Chapter 12 to add tables to a relationship. You will use it now to add the Orders and Products tables to the query.

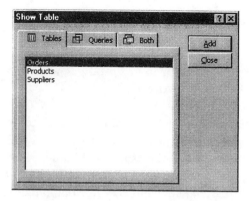

Figure 13.13 Show Table Dialogue Box

3.   Click on **Orders** and then click on **Add**.

4.   Click on **Products** and then click on **Add**, then click on **Close** ⊠ in the **Show Table** box. The Query Design window will appear.

You will now add the Quantity field from the Orders table to the query, and the Description and UnitPrice fields from the Products table. There are two ways to do this: you can either select them in the table or use drag and drop. You will try each of these methods in succession.

5.   Click in the **Table** row of the first column of the table in the bottom half of the screen. A down arrow appears to show that there is a drop-down list available.

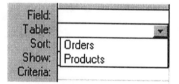

6.   Click on the down arrow and select the **Orders** table.

7.   Click in the **Field** row of the first column. Another down arrow appears.

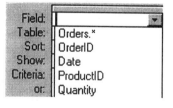

8.   Click on the down arrow and select the **Quantity** field.

Now you will add the Description field from the Products table using drag and drop.

9.   Click on the word **Description** where it appears in the list of fields in the **Products** table in the top half of the screen.

10.   Drag the mouse pointer down to the **Field** row of the second column of the table in the lower half of the screen and release the button.

11.   Add the **UnitPrice** field from the Products table to the query using either of the above methods. The resulting query is given in Figure 13.14.

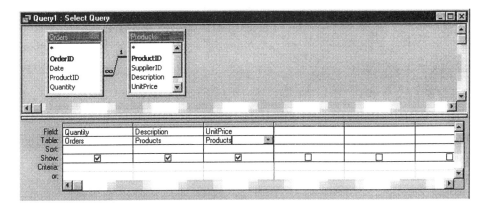

Figure 13.14 Resulting query

12.   Click on **Run** and you will see the screen in Figure 13.15.

13.   Click on the **Query View** icon to switch back to query design view.

Now that you have created the basic query, you can add criteria to it in exactly the same way as you did before. You can also add calculations, which you will do in Section 13.9.

Q6   How would you display all the orders except those for Beef or Pork sausages?

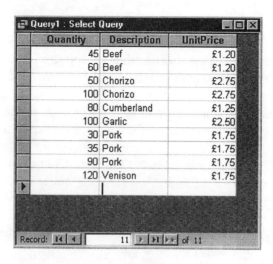

Figure 13.15 Query result

13.9 Adding calculations

The fields in a query do not all have to come from a database table. Access also lets you add *calculated* fields to a query. A calculated field is created by entering the expression that represents the calculation into an empty cell in the Field row. The name of the calculated field is specified by preceding the expression with a name and a colon (:). The arithmetic operators that can be used in expressions are:

* multiply	/ divide
+ add	– subtract

You will now add a calculation field to the query you created in Section 13.8. The new field will be used to calculated profits. The profit is 30% of the price, so it is calculated by multiplying the Unit Price by 0.3. The new field will be given the name Profit.

1. Click on the **Field** row of the first empty column of the query design table to position the cursor in the fourth column of the table.

2. Type the following expression into the new column:

Profit:[UnitPrice]*0.3

The first part of this expression **Profit:** shows that the new field is called

Profit, and the second part **[UnitPrice]*0.3** shows that it is calculated by multiplying the UnitPrice field by 0.3. Notice that square brackets [ ] must always be used when referring to field names such as UnitPrice in calculations.

3. Run the query, and you will see the screen in Figure 13.16, which has an extra column headed Profit. The values in this column are 30% of the values in the UnitPrice column.

4. Click on **Close** ✖ in the Query1: Select Query box, and you will be asked whether you want to save the query.

5. Click on **Yes**, then enter the query name **Profit** and click on **OK**. You will be returned to the database window.

Quantity	Description	UnitPrice	Profit
45	Beef	£1.20	0.36
60	Beef	£1.20	0.36
50	Chorizo	£2.75	0.825
100	Chorizo	£2.75	0.825
80	Cumberland	£1.25	0.375
100	Garlic	£2.50	0.75
30	Pork	£1.75	0.525
35	Pork	£1.75	0.525
90	Pork	£1.75	0.525
120	Venison	£1.75	0.525

Figure 13.16 Calculation query

6. Click on **Close** ✖ in the **Shop: database** window to close the database.

Q7 How would you add another field to the Profits query to calculate the total price of each order, which is calculated by multiplying the unit price by the quantity?

13.10 Summary

In this chapter you have been shown how to:

- Create queries to sort and filter data using either the **Query Wizard** or Query **Design View**.
- Use queries to extract data from more than one table at a time.

- Use queries to extract data from more than one table at a time.
- Use the comparison operators: $<, <=, >, >=, =, <>$.
- **Save** queries for future use.
- Combine different query criteria using **And** or **or**
- Perform calculations in queries using the arithmetic operators $*, /, +, -$.

13.11 Written exercises

13.11.1 The following questions refer to the Employees table in the Staff database that was created in Chapter 11. Explain what criteria you would add to a query to extract a list of each of the following:

a) All the employees aged over 40, apart from the one called Brook.

b) All the employees with salaries in the range £15,000–£25,000

c) All those who either have length of service above 10 years, or age below 40.

d) All the net salaries for each employee, where the net salary is 75% of the original salary.

13.11.2 Suppose that a university would like to collect some data from students for the purpose of course evaluation. The questionnaire in Figure 13.17 is issued to each student on each course. Each lecturer can teach many courses, but each course is only taught by one lecturer.

Course Title	
Prerequisites	
Term	
Year	
Lecturer Name	
Lecturer Title (Dr/Mr/Ms)	
Lecturer's Department	
Give each of the following course components a score out of 10:	
Lecturer	
Textbook	
Course content	
Tutorials	
Lecture handouts	

Figure 13.17 Lecturer questionnaire

Design a database in which to store all the data from the completed questionnaires. The data should be separated into three tables: Courses, Lecturers and Feedback. The Feedback table should hold the five scores from each questionnaire. Describe the relationships between the tables, assuming that each lecturer can teach several courses. Explain how you would design queries to produce the following data:

a) All the courses taught by a given lecturer.
b) All lecturers who have scored below 2 on any questionnaire.
c) The average of the five scores on each questionnaire.

13.12 Practical exercises

13.12.1 Open the **Shop** database, and make the following modifications:

a) Open the Suppliers table and change the value in the City field for supplier Scotts from Manchester to **Buckingham**. Open the SortedProducts query and see how it is affected by this change.

b) Create a new query called **FebruaryOrders** to list the Description, Date and Amount of all the orders made in February 1997.

c) Create a new query called **Discontinued** to list the Description and Supplier Names of all the discontinued products, but nothing else. In particular, the value of the Discontinued field should not be displayed.

d) Create a new query called **NetOrders** to list the OrderID, Date and NetAmount of each order. The NetAmount is 75% of the amount of each order, where the amount is calculated by multiplying the unit price by the quantity.

13.12.2 Design a database to be used by a mail order clothing company to keep a record of all its customers and the purchases they have made. The database should contain three tables. The first table should list all the customer information, such as the name and address of each customer. The second table should list all the product information, such as the price and current stock level of each product. The products should also be classified into different categories, such as Sports, Casual or Business clothes. The third table should list all the transactions made: it should list the products that have been sold to each customer, together with the date of the transaction. The three tables should be joined together by appropriate relationships. Design queries to perform the following tasks:

a) Produce a list of all the products with stock level below 100.

b) Produce a list of customer names and addresses for all the customers who have purchased some sports clothes in the last six months. It does not matter if the list contains duplicates.

c) Produce a Sale catalogue. This should list all the products that have a high stock level of over 1000. The price of each product in the Sale catalogue should be reduced to 60% of the original price.

13.12.3 Design a database to be used by a small arts centre to keep a record of all its customers and the performances they have attended. The database should contain three tables. The first table should list all the customer information, such as the name and address of each customer. It should also include a field to indicate whether the customer is entitled to concessions or not. The second table should contain a list of events, including the time, date and ticket price of each event, and the number of tickets that have not yet been sold. The third table should list how many tickets have been sold to each customer for each event. The three tables should be joined together by appropriate relationships. Design queries to perform the following tasks:

a) Produce a list of all the performances that are sold out.

b) Produce a list of the names and addresses of all the customers who have bought tickets for a particular film.

c) Produce a list of customer bills: the bill for each customer is calculated by multiplying the number of tickets sold to the customer by the price of each ticket.

14 Forms and Reports

14.1 Overview

A *form* is an alternative data entry method to a table. A *report* is used for data output. Both forms and reports can be created in similar ways. In this chapter you will cover the following topics:

- Creating a form with AutoForm.
- Adding data.
- Creating a form with the Form Wizard.
- Finding records.
- Creating a report with the Report Wizard.
- Modifying forms and reports in Design View.

14.2 Introduction

All the data in the databases you have created in the past has been typed directly into the database tables. This is not always the best way to enter data, since most tables contain too many fields to fit on a computer screen. Although it is possible to scroll through the table and view all the fields, it is usually more convenient to use a database form to enter data instead. A database form has a similar appearance to the kind of ordinary paper form that might be used in a variety of everyday situations. For example, many organisations would use a standard order form to order products from suppliers. In this chapter you will begin by creating the computerised equivalent of such a form within the Shop database. Order information can then be entered into the order form, and it will be automatically saved into the Orders table.

Forms are not necessarily based on a single table, since there are many situations where it is useful to enter data into several tables simultaneously. For example, if a user of the Shop database wanted to add an order for a new product they would need to add data to both the Orders and Products tables. In this chapter you will learn how to do this in a single database form.

Reports, like forms, display a selection of the fields of one or more database tables in a presentable format. The difference is that reports are designed specifically for data output rather than input: reports are usually printed out on paper. It is possible to print the data directly from any table, query or form, but the results will not look as professional as those produced by a report.

14.3 Creating a form using AutoForm

There are three ways to create a form: AutoForm, Form Wizard and Form Design View. AutoForm is quick, but has no flexibility: all the fields from a table or query are added to the form. The Form Wizard is more flexible. It allows you to select which fields to add to the form, in the same way that the Query Wizard allows you to select fields to add to a query. Form Design View offers the most flexibility.

You will start by creating a form with AutoForm. The form you will create will have a *Columnar* layout, which means that all the fields will appear in a column on the screen. The other layout styles are *Tabular* and *Datasheet*. Forms with these layouts display all the same information in a slightly different way. A form can be based on any table or query. Forms based on queries can be used to combine data from separate tables. Follow the steps below to create a columnar form based on the Orders table.

1. Start up Access and open the **Shop** database.

2. Click the **Forms** tab, then click on the **New** button and you will see the New Form dialogue box in Figure 14.1.

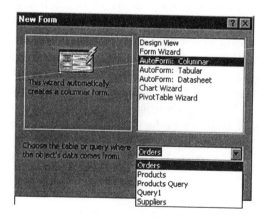

Figure 14.1 New form dialogue box

3.   Click **AutoForm: Columnar**, then click on the down-arrow at the bottom of the dialogue box to open the drop-down list of tables and queries, and select **Orders**.

4.   Click on **OK** and the form shown in Figure 14.2 will appear.

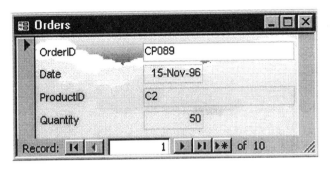

Figure 14.2 Orders form

The form shows all the data from a single record: the first record of the Orders table. Each of the fields appears one below another because the form has a columnar layout. In section 14.4 you will see how to use this form to display other records in the Orders table.

14.4 Viewing records in a form

The Orders form only displays the data from one record of the Orders table at a time. The icons at the bottom of the Orders form can be used to move through the Orders table and display other records. The box between the Previous and Next record buttons shows the number of the current record being displayed in the table. These icons are the same as the ones used to control the display of database tables and are listed in Figure 14.3. You will try out some of these buttons below.

I◄	First record
◄	Previous record
►	Next record
►I	Last record
►✳	New record

Figure 14.3 Table navigation icons

1. Click on ▶ to view the next record in the table. Then click on ▶ several more times to see some of the other records.

2. Click on ◀ to move to the previous record.

Q1   Use the icons to move through the Orders table until you reach record number 5. What is its OrderID?

14.5 Entering data

The main reason for creating a form is to provide an easy way to enter data into a database. You will now use the Orders form to add a new record to the Orders table, and then close and save the form.

1. Click on ▶* to insert a new record. A blank form will appear.

2. Type text **JC046** into the OrderID box of the form, then press **Tab** or **Enter** and the cursor will move down to the Date box.

3. Enter the value **11-Dec-97** for the Date, **B1** for the ProductID and **150** for the Quantity. If you press Enter after you have typed in the amount,another blank form will appear ready for more data entry, but you will not add any more data at this stage (see Figure 14.4).

4. Click on **Close** ☒ in the Orders Form window and you will be asked if you want to save the changes to Form1, which is the default name given to the form you have created.

5. Click on **Yes** and you will see the familiar Save As box, with the default form name **Orders**. Click on **OK** to save the form to this name and return to the database window.

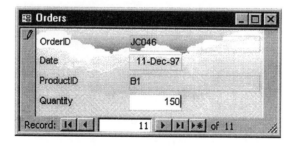

Figure 14.4 Sample data input

14.6 Creating a form with the Form Wizard

The Orders form you created in Section 14.4 is not ideal. The problem is that the only reference to the product being ordered is to its ProductID. This number may be difficult to remember. Also, you may wish to add the details of a new product to the database at the same time as adding an order. It would be useful if the product details could appear on the form as well, but these are stored in the Products table, not the Orders table. So you need to create a new form that includes fields from both tables.

One way to add fields from two tables to a form is to use the Form Wizard. Another way is to create a query based on the two tables and then use either AutoForm or the Form Wizard to create the form from the query rather than the underlying tables. You will now use the Form Wizard to create a form based on the Orders and Products tables.

1. Select the **Forms** tab if it not still selected, then click on the **New** button.

2. Select **Form Wizard** and click on **OK**. There is no need to select a table from the drop-down list, because this form will be based on two tables, so the selection will be made at a later stage.

3. Select **Table: Orders** from the **Tables/Queries** drop-down box if it is not already selected.

4. Click the ▶▶ button to add all the fields in the **Available Fields** column to the **Selected Fields** column.

5. Select the **ProductID** field, then click the ◀ button to remove it from the **Selected Fields** column. You do not need to add the ProductID field to the form yet, because it is also part of the Products table and will be added from there.

6. Select **Table: Products** from the **Tables/Queries** drop-down box.

7. Click on the ▶▶ button again to add all the fields in the **Available Fields** column to the **Selected Fields** list.

8. Click **Next** and you will see the screen in Figure 14.5.

There are two ways that the data in your form can be viewed, since it is based on two tables. If you view the data by Products, then each form will display the product details at the top of the form, followed by all the orders for that product. If you view the data by Orders, then each form will contain only one order, together with its product details. Your table will be viewed by Products.

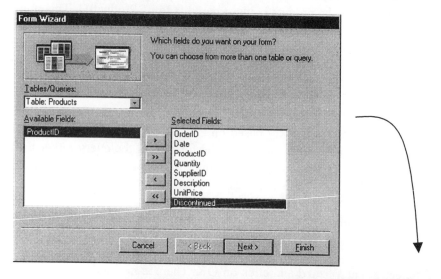

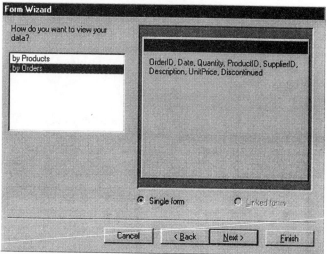

Figure 14.5 Form Wizard box

9.   Select **by Products**, then click **Next** again, and you will be asked which layout you would like for your form.

10. Click on each of the buttons to see a preview of each of the layout styles, and select **Datasheet** as the layout style for your form.

11. Click **Next** again and you will see the screen in Figure 14.6. The screen allows you to select a background style for the form.

12. Click on some of the different styles in the window on the right to see how the preview on the left changes.

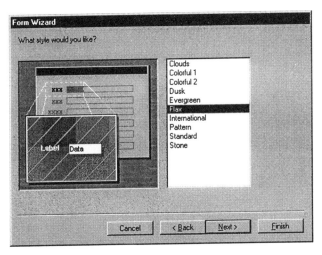

Figure 14.6 Form Wizard background style box

13. Select **Flax** and click on **Next** again. You will be asked what name you want to give your form and subform. You need two names because the form you are creating will generate two forms: one containing all the orders, and another containing both products and orders.

14. Click on **Finish** to accept the default names of **Products** and **Orders Subform** for the two forms. The screen shown in Figure 14.7 will appear.

Data can be entered into both the Products and Orders tables using this form.

14.7 Entering data

Figure 14.7 shows two navigation bars: one for Orders and one for Products. New records can be inserted into either table using the appropriate bar. You will start by inserting a new order.

1. Click on the ▶ button in the **Products** navigation bar to see all the orders for the next product: Cocktail sausage.

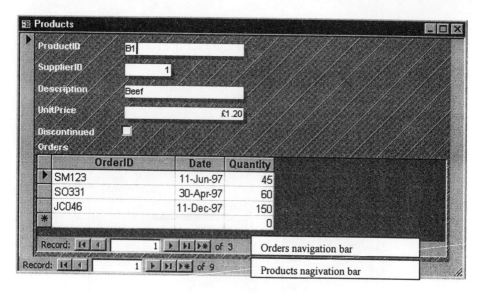

Figure 14.7 Products form

2.   Keep pressing the ▶ button on the Products navigation until you reach the list of orders for **Pork** sausages (see Figure 14.8).

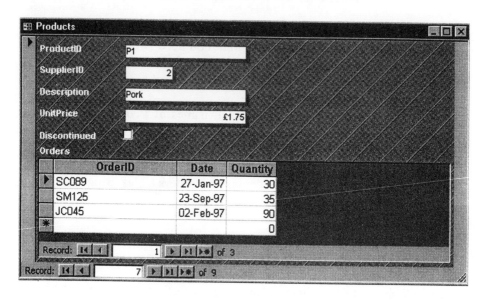

Figure 14.8 Products form

Q2   What happens when you click on the ▶ *button on the Orders naviga-tion bar?*

3. Click on the New Record icon **▶*** in the **Orders** navigation bar to insert a new order for Pork sausages. The cursor will move to the blank row at the bottom of the Orders subform.

4. Enter the OrderID **SC022**, Date **1-Dec-97** and Quantity **70**.

Now you will insert a new product.

5. Click on the New Record icon **▶*** in the **Products** navigation bar. A blank form will appear.

6. Enter a new product with ProductID **V2**, SupplierID **5**, Description **Vegetarian** and UnitPrice **£1.10**. You will not add any orders for this product at the moment.

7. Click on **Close ☒** in the Products Form window to return to the database window.

14.8 Finding records

One problem with entering or modifying data in a form is that it can be difficult to locate records. One way to find records is to use the *Find* feature. Follow the steps below to find all the orders with a given ProductID.

1. Open the **Orders** form.

2. Click on the **ProductID** field.

3. Select **Edit, Find** or click on the **Find** icon 🔍. You will see the Find dialogue box shown in Figure 14.9.

The title bar shows the field name ProductID to indicate that the cursor was in this field when the Find command was selected. There are a number of options that can be set to control the search you are about to perform. For example, the Search option can be set to All, Up or Down to search the whole table, or just backwards or forwards from the current position. The Match option can be used to control whether the search text is matched with the whole field or just part of it.

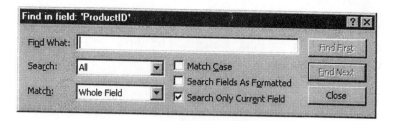

Figure 14.9 Find dialogue box

4. Type the identifier **B1** into the **Fi<u>n</u>d What** box to search for records with ProductID B1.

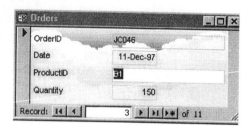

5. Click on **Find First** to find the first record with this product identifier. The record will appear in the Orders form.

6. Click on **Find Next** search for the next record with the same product identifier.

7. Keep clicking on **Find Next** until you see the message box in Figure 14.10.

8. Click on **OK**, then click on **Close** ✕ in the Find dialogue box.

9. Click on **Close** ✕ in the Orders form.

Q3   *How do you think you would use the Find feature to search for all the orders with OrderID beginning with the letters SM?*

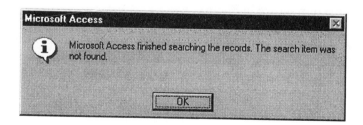

Figure 14.10 Message box

14.9 Creating a report

The main purpose of a report is to output all or part of the contents of a database in a readable form. Reports are often based on queries because they are usually used to output selective information in some chosen format. For example, a report might be used in the Shop database to output an alphabetical list of all the products made by British suppliers. In this section you will create a report based on the SortedProducts query you created in Chapter 13.

There are a number of ways to create reports including AutoReport, Report Wizard and Report Design View. Each of these methods is similar to the corresponding method for forms, so you will only use one method here: the Report Wizard.

1. Click the **Reports** tab, then click on the **New** button and you will see the New Report dialogue box in Figure 14.11.

2. Click **Report Wizard** and click on **OK**. There is no need to select a table from the drop-down list at this stage.

3. Select **Query: SortedProfits** from the **Tables/Queries** drop-down box.

4. Use the [button image] button to add the fields **SupplierName**, **UnitPrice**, and **Description** from the **Available Fields** column to the **Selected Fields** column.

5. Click **Next** and you will be asked how you want to view your data. Leave the selection on **by Suppliers**.

6. Click **Next** and you will be asked if you want any grouping levels. If you choose to group the data by one or more of the fields in the report, then all the records with a common value in that field will be grouped together. In this case you will accept the default option of no grouping.

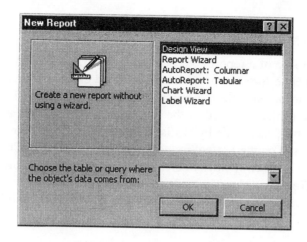

Figure 14.11 New Report dialogue box

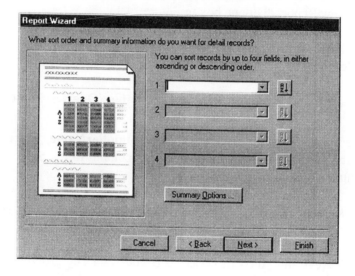

Figure 14.12 Report Wizard sorting dialogue box

7.   Click **Next** and you will see the screen in Figure 14.12.

This screen allows you to sort the report in a number of ways. You will sort it into increasing order of unit price.

8.   Click on the down arrow in the box marked 1 to see the drop-down list and select **UnitPrice** from the list. Click **Next** and you will be asked how you want to layout your report. Click on some of the different options and see how the preview changes.

9.   Select **Stepped,** then click on **Next** and you will be asked what style

you want for the report. Click on some of the different options and see how the preview changes.

10. Select **Compact**, then click **Next** again, and you will be asked how you want to name the report.

11. Change the default name of Suppliers to **Products** and click on **Finish**. The screen shown in Figure 14.13 will appear.

12. Change the setting of the **Zoom** box 100% [img] on the toolbar to **75%** to make the report more readable. And use the scroll bar on the right of the screen to move down the report. Notice that the report is grouped into orders from each supplier, because you chose to view it by Supplier. Notice also that the orders are sorted into increasing order of Unit Price.

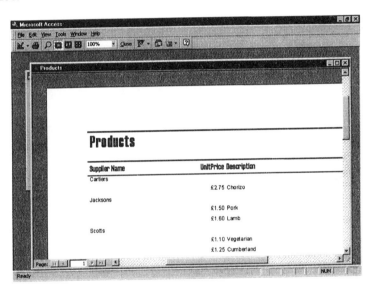

Figure 14.13 Products report

14.10 Printing and closing reports

1. Click on the **Print** icon [printer icon] or select **File**, **Print** then **OK** to print the report in the usual way.

2. Click on **Close** [X] in the Products Report window to close the report.

14.11 Modifying forms and reports

Forms and reports can both be created and viewed in design view, just like tables and queries. Design view can be used to add fields to the form or report, or to remove them. It can also be used to move and resize fields and to add extra formatting features such as titles and pictures. Since the techniques for modifying forms and reports in design view are very similar, you will not do both here. In this section you will make some minor changes to the Products report created in Section 14.9 in order to gain familiarity with report Design view.

1.   Click the **Reports** tab, and select the **Products** report if it is not still selected.

2.   Click the **Design** button. You will see the screen in Figure 14.14.

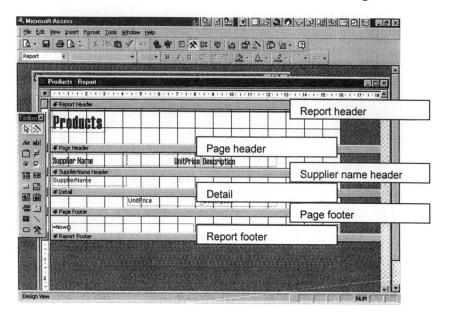

Figure 14.14 Profits report

This screen shows the Products report in design view. This view of the report can be used to change its format, and add or delete fields if necessary. The screen is divided into six sections, which are described briefly below:

- *Report Header*: appears once at the top of the report.
- *Page Header*: appears at the top of every page.
- *Supplier Name Header*: controls the position of the supplier name.

- *Detail*: controls the position of fields in the main body of the report.
- *Page Footer*: appears at the bottom of every page.
- *Report Footer*: appears at the bottom of the report.

You will modify the Page Header and the Detail sections of the Products report in order to move the Description column to the right of the report. You will begin with the header.

3. Click on the word **Description** in the **Page Header** section of the report. Small black squares will appear round the Description box to show that it has been selected.

4. Position the mouse pointer on one of the border lines round the Description box, so that the pointer turns into a small black hand.

5. Click and drag the box to the right.

6. Click on the **Report View** icon or select **View**, **Print Preview** to see how the report has changed.

The Description header has been shifted to the right, but the product descriptions are no longer correctly aligned below it. You will now move those to the right as well.

7. Select **View, Design View** to return to design view.

8. Click on the word **Description** in the **Detail** section of the report to select it.

9. Drag the box to the right as you did before so that it is aligned below the Description box in the Page Header section.

10. Click on the **Report View** icon again to see how the report has changed.

11. Click on **Close** in the Products Report window, then click on **Yes** to save the changes to the report.

Q4   *Open the Orders form in Design View. Explain how to move the OrderID field up higher in the form to separate it from the rest of the fields.*

12. Click on **Close** in the Shop: database main window.

14.12 Summary

In this chapter you have been shown how to do the following:

- Use **AutoForm** and **Form Wizard** to create forms based on one or more tables or queries.
- Use forms to enter data into tables.
- Find records to view in a form using **Edit, Find**.
- Use the **Report Wizard** to create a report for displaying selected data in a readable format.

14.13 Written exercises

14.13.1   Use the Shop database to answer the questions below.

a) When would the columnar layout for forms be more useful than the tabular?

b) Explain how you would create a report containing the fields OrderID, Date and Quantity from the Orders table, sorted in increasing order of date.

c) How would you create a report to display all the products that have been discontinued.

d) Describe two different ways to create a report containing the SupplierName and Country fields from the Suppliers table, and the ProductID field from the Products table.

14.13.2   Change the setting of the **Zoom** box on the toolbar to **75%** to make the report more readable. And use the scroll bar on the right of the screen to move down the report. Notice that the report is grouped into orders from each supplier, because you chose to view it by Supplier. Notice also that the orders are sorted into increasing order of Unit Price. Design a simple database to be used by a legal company to store information about its clients, such as the court cases that have been fought on their behalf, and the outcomes of those cases. Your design should show all the tables to be included in the database, and the relationships between them. It should also list the forms in the database, stating clearly which fields are included in each form. You should include some queries in your design, and some reports based either on queries or tables.

14.14 Practical exercises

14.14.1 Design a database to be used by a bank to keep a record of all its customers and the transactions they have made. The database should include a table called Branches, to list information about all the different branches of the bank. It should have another table called Customers, to list all the customer details. Assume that each customer can only have an account at one branch, so create a one-to-many relationship between Branches and Customers. Create a third table, called Transactions to store all the customer transactions and set up an appropriate relationship between Customers and Transactions. Create any other tables and relationships you consider necessary. Create at least three forms for your database. One of the forms should contain fields from the Customers and Transactions tables together, with the Transactions data appearing on a subform of the Customers form. Your database should also include some reports, including the following two which must be based on queries.

a) All the transactions at one of the branches, sorted in order of date.

b) All the transactions exceeding £1000 made by one of the customers during a given month.

14.14.2 Create a new database for storing information about food and wine. Use the **Table Wizard** to create the following three tables in the database. These tables all come from the list of **Personal** Sample Tables, not the Business ones.

a) **Categories.** Include both fields. Add the following categories to the table: Desert, Poultry, Red Meat, Vegetables, Fish, Other.

b) **Recipes.** Include the fields: RecipeID, RecipeName, FoodCategoryID, Vegetarian, Ingredients and Instructions. Rename the FoodCategoryID field to CategoryID, either in the Table Wizard or in Design View. Do not add any data to the table yet.

c) **WineList**. Include the fields: WineListID, WineName, WineTypeID and CountryOfOrigin. Rename the WineTypeID field to CategoryID. Do not add any data to the table yet.

14.14.3 Create relationships between the Categories and Recipes tables, and between the Categories and WineList tables, using the CategoryID field. Add two forms to the database: one for the Recipes table, and one for the WineList table. Use the forms to add some data to each table. Your database should also include some reports, including the following two which must be based on queries.

a) A list of vegetarian recipes.

b) All the wines that are in either the Poultry or Red Meat categories.

14.14.4 Create a simple database to be used by a doctor's surgery to store information about its patients, doctors, nurses and ailments. The database should include all the database features covered in this book: tables, relationships, queries, forms and reports.

15 Introduction to PowerPoint

15.1 Overview

In this chapter you will learn how to create presentations based on predesigned templates in PowerPoint. You will then perform some very simple manipulations on one of the presentations. You will cover the following features of PowerPoint:

- Creating a presentation with the AutoContent Wizard.
- Saving.
- Changing views.
- Printing.
- Closing a presentation.
- Creating a presentation with a Presentation template.
- Simple editing.
- Simple animation.

15.2 Introduction

There are many situations when it is useful to produce a polished presentation. PowerPoint can be used to create presentations in each of the following formats:

- On screen presentation.
- Black and white overheads.
- Colour overheads.
- 35 mm slides.

An on screen presentation is the most flexible, since it can include sound and animation effects as well as ordinary text and graphics. It is not always convenient to show a presentation directly on the computer though, so it is often preferable to produce overhead projector slides. A third alternative is to produce 35 mm slides for display on a slide projector, but these must be converted by a special service bureau.

201

There are three ways to create a presentation in PowerPoint:

- *AutoContent Wizard* allows you to select the presentation topic and style options from a variety of built in designs. The resulting presentation contains sample text that can be edited to suit your requirements.
- *Templates* are of two types: *Presentation Design* and *Presentation*. A presentation design template provides a general layout and style for the slides, but no sample text. A presentation template contains style information and sample text identical to that produced by the AutoContent Wizard. It is a less flexible method for creating presentations than the Wizard, since it assumes all the default settings apart from the topic.
- *Blank Presentation* can be used to create a presentation from scratch.

In this chapter you will create presentations using the first two of these methods. The third method will be covered in Chapter 16.

Once a presentation has been created, it can be viewed in a number of different ways. So for example, it is possible to view the contents of a number of consecutive slides simultaneously. This can be particularly useful for editing the text in the slides. The slides can also be printed in a number of different ways, which can be useful for producing summaries and handouts. Each of the different viewing and printing methods will be described fully in this chapter.

15.3 Starting PowerPoint

1. Click on the **Start** button, then point to the **Programs** icon and click on **Microsoft PowerPoint**. Alternatively, double-click on the PowerPoint icon 📇. You will see a dialogue box similar to that in Figure 15.1.

The three ways to create a presentation in PowerPoint were described in Section 15.2. Normally, you would either open an existing presentation or create a new one when you see this screen, but first we will examine the PowerPoint toolbar.

2. Click on **Cancel** and the screen will clear to look like that in Figure 15.2.

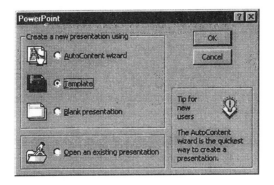

Figure 15.1 PowerPoint start up window

The PowerPoint screen contains the standard Windows menus, toolbars, status bar and Help options. You can find out what each toolbar button does by pointing at it with your mouse pointer in the usual way. There are some buttons on the PowerPoint toolbar that do not appear on other Windows programs, such as the *Increase Font Size* button.

Q1　*What does the Decrease Font Size button look like?*

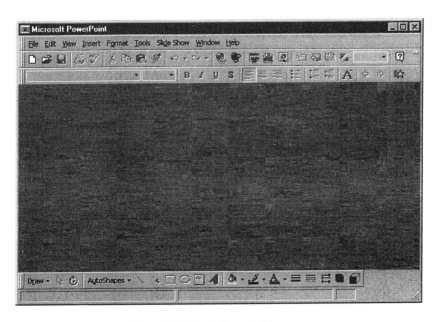

Figure 15.2 Blank PowerPoint screen

You will create two presentations in this chapter, both of which will contain sample text guidelines to help you structure your presentation. The first will be created with the AutoContent Wizard, and the second with a Presentation template. The steps for using the AutoContent Wizard are quite different in Office 97 and Office Version 7, so make sure you follow the steps marked *Version 7* if you are using the older version of Office.

1.   Select **File, New** from the menu. The screen will look like that in Figure 15.3.

2.   Click the **Presentations** tab if it is not already selected.

3.   Double click on **AutoContent Wizard** to start the Wizard.

4.   Click **Next** when the first screen of the Wizard appears.

Version 7   Enter your name and type the text *A Strategy for Education* for the subject of your presentation. Type the current date into the box for other information. Then click on **Next**.

5.   Select **Recommending a Strategy** for the type of presentation if it is not already selected, then click **Next**.

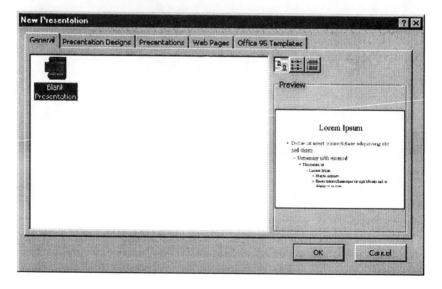

Figure 15.3 New Presentation screen

6. Click **Next** to accept the default settings on the next screen.

7. You will then be asked what kind of output you require. Select **Colour Overheads**, and click **Next**. Note that the left half of the dialogue box shows your current position in the AutoContent Wizard path.

Version 7   Omit the next step if you are using Office 7.

8. Give your presentation the title *A Strategy for Education*, then enter your name, and give the current date as additional information.

9. Click **Finish** and you will see the screen in Figure 15.4.

Version 7   In Version 7, the presentation will appear in Slide View, and will not look like that in Figure 15.4. Select **View, Outline** to see this screen.

The screen shows the *Outline View* of the presentation. This view shows the contents of all the slides in a concise form which is easy to edit. At the moment the text in the slides consists of guidelines to help you structure your presentation. You will see how to preview the slides as they will appear in the presentation in Section 15.6, after you have saved your presentation.

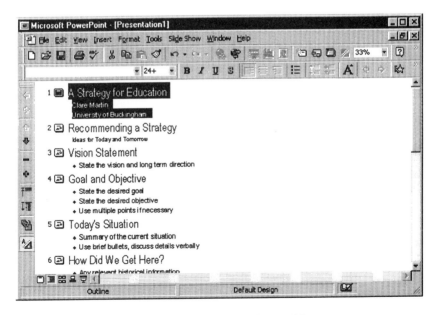

Figure 15.4 Presentation in Outline View

15.5 Saving a presentation

The method for saving a presentation is the same as that for saving any other Microsoft Windows application, as shown in the steps below.

1. Select **File, Save** from the menu, or click on the **Save** icon ▦. You will see the standard Save dialogue box.

2. Set the **Save in** option to the folder in which you want to save your presentation, by clicking the down arrow ▼ on the right of the Save in box and selecting an option. If you are using a floppy disk, insert it into the drive and select the **3½ Floppy (A:)** option.

3. Set the **File name** option to **Strategy** and click on **Save**.

The extension **ppt** will be added to the filename automatically, so the full name of the database file is **Strategy.ppt**, but the extension **ppt** will not always be displayed.

15.6 Viewing the slides

The quickest way to change the appearance of the slides is to use the *View buttons* shown in Figure 15.5.

Follow the steps below to try out each of the different views. You will begin with *Slide Show* view, which allows you to see what the slides will look like, but you will not be able to edit them at all.

1. Click on the **Slide Show** button shown in Figure 15.5, or select **View, Slide Show**. The first slide of the presentation will appear, as shown in Figure 15.6.

2. Click on the **right mouse button** to see the list of options in Figure 15.7.

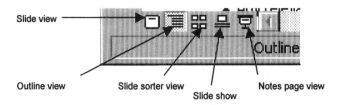

Figure 15.5 View buttons

Version 7 The list of options in Version 7 is slightly different.

3.	Select **Next** to see the next slide in the presentation, or press the **Page Down** key. Alternatively, click on the left mouse button to move through the slides.

4.	Click on the right mouse button, and select **Next** a few more times to see some more of the slides.

Figure 15.6 Slide 1 of presentation

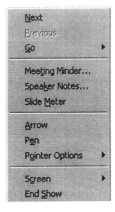

Figure 15.7 Slide navigation options

5. Click on the right mouse button followed by **End Show** to finish look-ing at the slide show and return to Outline view.

If you want to see what the slides will look like, and wish to edit them at the same time, you can use the *Slide* view. You will try this out in the steps be-low, but you will not edit any of the slides until Section 15.10.

6. Click on the **1** next to the title *A Strategy for Education* to select the first slide of the presentation if it is not already selected.

7. Click on the **Slide View** button shown in Figure 15.5, or select **View, Slide**. The first slide of the presentation will appear as it did in Figure 15.7, but this time the slide will not fill the whole computer screen. It will be surrounded by the usual menus and toolbars to facilitate editing.

8. Click on the down arrow ![down arrow] on the scroll bar at the right of the screen to see the next slide.

9. Drag the small rectangle on the right-hand scroll bar down a short way to jump forward to a later slide.

When you have finished using the scroll bar to move through some of the slides, you can change to *Slide Sorter* view to get a more general overview of the slide show.

10. Click on the **Slide Sorter View** button shown in Figure 15.5, or select **View, Slide Sorter**. The presentation will appear in Slide Sorter view as shown in Figure 15.8.

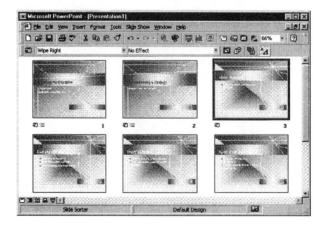

Figure 15.8 Slide Sorter view

The last way to view the slides is in Notes Pages view. In this view each slide is displayed together with a space for adding the speaker's notes. This can be useful if you want to make notes to accompany the presentation. Follow the steps below to view one of the slides in Notes view.

11. Click on one of the slides to select it. A dark border will appear round the selected slide.

12. Click on the **Notes Page View** button shown in Figure 15.5, or select **View**, **Notes Page**. The current slide will appear in Notes Page view as shown in Figure 15.9.

You can add notes to the slide by clicking the lower half of the screen, and then typing the notes. If the notes are difficult to read then you may wish to select a higher value for the Zoom control on the toolbar (54% ▼).

You will learn how to make changes to the text in a presentation in Section 15.10, but first you will print and close this one.

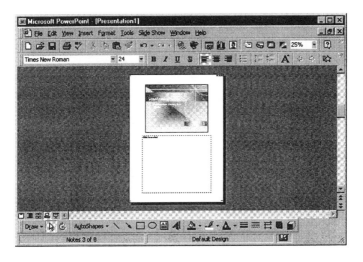

Figure 15.9 Notes Page view

15.7 Printing a presentation

There are a number of different ways to print out a presentation, corresponding to the different ways of viewing slides:

- *Slides* Each slide is printed in landscape orientation, which means that the wide edge of the paper is at the top of the printout. Each slide is printed on a separate page.
- *Outline View* The outline description of the slides is printed.
- *Handouts* The slides are printed with two, three, or six on each page.
- *Notes Page* Each slide is printed on a separate page, with notes below it.

Follow the steps below to print out Handouts for the Strategy presentation, with six slides per page.

1.　　Select **File**, **Print** and you will see the screen in Figure 15.10.

2.　　Click on the down arrow in the **Print what** box to see a drop-down list of the different ways to print slides.

3.　　Select **Handouts (6 slides per page)** and click on **OK**.

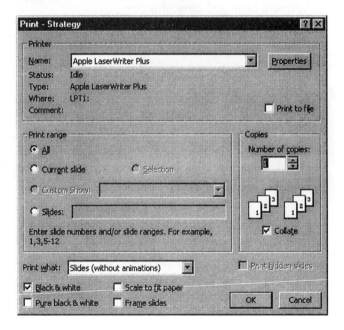

Figure 15.10 Print options

15.8　Closing a presentation

1.　　Close the presentation by clicking the **Close** ✕ button on the inner window.

15.9 Creating a presentation using a presentation template

The quickest way to create a presentation is to use a Presentation Template. The reason that it is quicker to use a template rather than the AutoContent Wizard is that templates assume all the default design options, so the resulting presentation has a very standard format. Follow the steps below to create a new presentation from a template.

1.   Select **File, New** from the menu.

2.   Click the **Presentations** tab if it is not already selected.

3.   Double click on **Company Meeting (Standard)** to create the presentation. The first slide will appear in Slide view.

Version 7   The presentation is just called **Company Meeting** in Office 7.

4.   Click on the **Outline View** button to see the full contents of the presentation.

15.10 Simple editing in outline view

Both the presentations you have created in this chapter contain guiding text to help you structure your presentation. This text must be edited to produce the final presentation. In this chapter you will just try out some basic techniques: editing text, deleting slides and changing background. Further editing topics are covered in Chapter 16.

1.   Delete the word **Presenter** in the first slide and replace it with your own name.

2.   Select slide number 3 by clicking the slide icon ⬜ next to the number 3. All the text from the slide will be highlighted.

3.   Delete slide 3 by pressing the **Delete** key on the keyboard, or selecting **Edit, Delete Slide**. The slide will be removed.

You will now change the background design that appears on the slide.

4.   Select **Format, Apply Design** or click on the **Apply Design** icon ▣. You will see the screen in Figure 15.11.

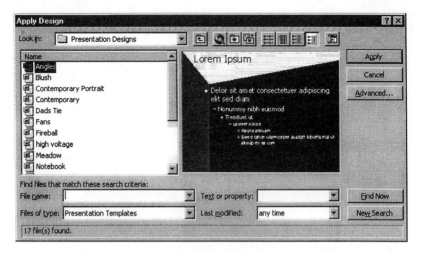

Figure 15.11 Apply Design screen

5. Click on a template name in the **Name** list on the left of the screen. A preview of the design will appear on the right of the screen.

6. Choose a template name, and then click on the **Apply** button. You will return to Outline view.

7. Click on the **Slide View** button to see the effects of the new template in Slide view.

15.11 Simple animation effects

There are two different kinds of simple animation affect that can be added to a presentation: *Transition* effects and *Text Preset Animation* effects. Transition effects are used to animate the movement of one slide to the next. Text Preset Animation effects are used to animate the appearance of text, such as bullet points within each slide. You will begin by adding some transition effects to all of the slides in your presentation.

1. Select **Slide Sorter View** and you will see the Transition Effects and Text Preset Animation Effects boxes shown in Figure 15.12.

Version 7 Text Preset Animation effects are called Text Build Effects.

2. Select all of the slides using **Edit, Select All**.

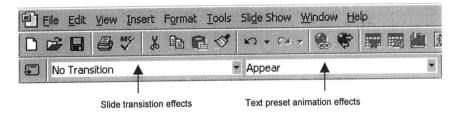

Slide transistion effects   Text preset animation effects

Figure 15.12 Animation effects

3. Click the down arrow on the **Transition Effects** box to see the list of transition effects available.

4. Select **Checkerboard Across**.

5. Select **Slide Show** to see each slide in full, and click on the left mouse button to move through some of the slides in the presentation and see the effects of the checkerboard animation.

Now you will add some text animation effects to your presentation to animate the appearance of the bullet points on the screen.

6. Return to **Slide Sorter View**.

7. Select all of the slides again using **Edit, Select All**.

8. Click the down arrow on the **Text Preset Animation** box to see the list of effects available.

9. Select **Fly From Right**.

10. Select **Slide Show** to see the slides in full again, and click on the left mouse button to move through some of the slides in the presentation to see the effects of the text animation. Each of the bullet points on the slide will fly in from the right one by one as you click on the mouse.

11. **Exit** from Slide Show view again.

15.12 Closing PowerPoint

1. Select **File, Save** or click on the **Save** icon to save the presentation.

2. Set the **Save in** to the folder in which you want your presentation and set the **File name** to **Company**, then click on **Save**.

3. Close the presentation by clicking on the **Close** ⊠ button in the inner window, then close PowerPoint by clicking on its **Close** ⊠ button.

15.13 Summary

In this chapter you have been shown how to do the following:

*   Create a presentation using the **AutoContent Wizard** or **Presentation Design**.
*   View presentations in several different ways: **Slide, Outline, Notes Page, Slide Sorter** or **Slide View**.
*   Print presentations in several different ways, corresponding to the different views.
*   Add simple animation using **Transition** effects and **Text Preset Animation** effects.

15.14 Written exercises

15.14.1 Describe some of the differences between the standard Word and PowerPoint toolbars.

15.14.2 Briefly explain the differences between the various ways to view slides in PowerPoint.

15.15 Practical exercises

15.15.1 Use the AutoContent Wizard to create an on screen presentation based on the template called **Training**. Give your presentation a title of your choice, and enter your name so that it will appear on the title page. Then make the following modifications to the presentation:

*   Use the **Apply Design** feature to change the background design of the slides.
*   Delete all except the first four slides.

- Change the text in the remaining slides so that it is relevant to the title subject you have chosen.
- Print out the slides in Slide view.

15.15.2 Create a presentation on any subject using either the AutoContent Wizard or a Presentation Design template. Modify the text to suit your purpose, then print it out in Slide Sorter view.

16 Designing a Presentation

16.1 Overview

In this chapter you will learn how to create a presentation in PowerPoint, without using a predesigned template. You will also learn how to share information between the different parts of Microsoft Office. You will cover the following features of PowerPoint:

- Creating a presentation from scratch.
- Editing in Outline and Slide view.
- Adding pictures.
- The drawing toolbar.
- More animation effects.
- Copying between applications.

16.2 Introduction

All of the presentations you have created so far have been based on presentation templates, so the text has been added by editing the guidelines on the template. In this chapter you will learn how to create a presentation starting from scratch. This is useful if your presentation does not fit into any of the presentation template categories. You will also learn how to edit a presentation in slide view, instead of outline view. This is particularly useful for enhancing the appearance of slides by including graphics and formatting features.

The final topic of this chapter connects all the parts of Microsoft Office that have been covered in this book. There are a number of different ways to share information between applications, varying from the more advanced object linking techniques to simple drag and drop. Object linking allows files to be linked together in such a way that any changes to one file automatically cause the other file to be updated. This topic is beyond the scope of this book. Instead, we will focus on the simpler techniques which are still very valuable.

16.3 Creating a blank presentation

1. If PowerPoint is not already running, then start it up the same way that you did in the previous chapter and click **Cancel** when you see the PowerPoint start up screen shown previously in Figure 15.1.

2. Select **File**, **New** from the menu, then click on the **General** tab if it is not already selected.

3. Double click on the **Blank Presentation** icon and you will see the New Slide dialogue box shown in Figure 16.1.

This screen allows you to select a general layout for your slides. Normally, you should choose a layout that matches the content of most of your slides. For example, if most slides will include a picture then the layout in the bottom left corner might be the best.

Q1 Which layout would be the best if most slides must contain an Excel chart?

4. Select the **AutoLayout** in the top left-hand corner, which is highlighted in Figure 16.1, and click **OK**.

5. A blank slide will appear in Slide view, as shown in Figure 16.2.

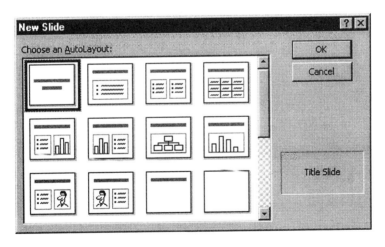

Figure 16.1 New Slide dialogue box

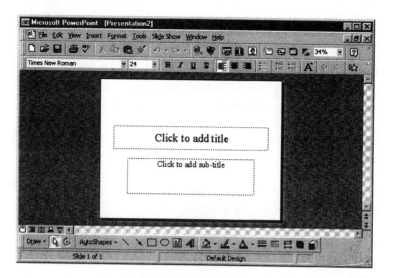

Figure 16.2 Blank slide

There are two areas for adding text into this slide, because of the AutoLayout you selected. A different AutoLayout would result in a different blank slide layout, which might include an area for a bulleted list, or a picture for example. Unlike the presentations you created in Chapter 15, which contained guidelines for adding text, this one is empty. You will add some text to the presentation in Section 16.4.

16.4   Adding text

The easiest way to add text to a presentation is to use Outline view. The slides can then be made more visually appealing in Slide view, and notes can be added in Notes Page view.

1.   Click on the **Outline View** button or select **View, Outline** to switch to Outline view. A blank screen will appear like that in Figure 16.3.

Q2 What is the difference between the toolbars of Figures 16.2 and 16.3?

The presentation that you will create is shown in Figure 16.4. It contains some information about the University of Buckingham which might be of interest to prospective students.

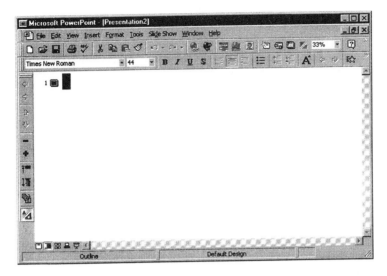

Figure 16.3 Blank presentation in Outline view

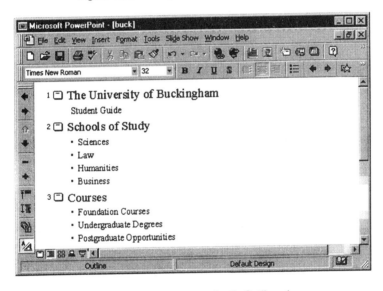

Figure 16.4 New presentation in Outline view

2. Type the first heading: **The University of Buckingham** onto the blank slide in Outline view, and press **Enter**. The screen will look like that in Figure 16.5. You will need to use two of the icons on the left toolbar to add the subheading to the first slide, since it is at a lower level than the main heading. These icons are shown below:

➡ *Demote* This button changes a heading to a lower level.

⬅ *Promote* This button changes a heading to a higher level.

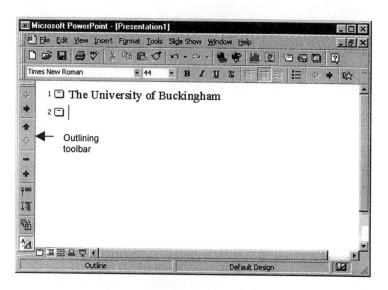

Figure 16.5 First Heading in Outline view

3. Press the **Demote** button to add the subheading, then type the text **Student Guide** and press **Enter**.

4. Press the **Promote** button to begin the next slide, and type the next heading: **Schools of Study**. Then press **Enter**. The screen will look like that in Figure 16.6.

5. Press the **Demote** button to add the subheading, and a bullet point • will automatically appear. Type the text **Sciences** next to it. Bullet points automatically appear on indented text on all slides except the first one.

6. Continue to add all the text shown in Figure 16.4, then **Save** the presentation to the file named **Buckingham** on your floppy disk.

7. Click on slide number **1** to move the cursor back to the beginning of the presentation.

8. Click on the **Slide Show** icon ⊡ at the bottom of the screen to see a preview of the first slide. Then click on the **mouse** button or press **Page Down** to preview the next two slides before returning to Outline view.

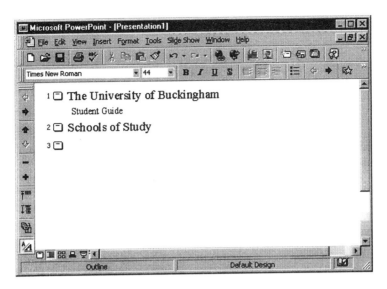

Figure 16.6 First slide in Outline view

16.5   Copying and moving slides in outline view

The techniques for copying and moving slides in PowerPoint are similar to those in each of the other parts of the Office suite. Slides can be moved using either cut and paste or drag and drop, as well as with the special icons on the PowerPoint toolbar. You will practise each of these three methods for moving or copying in turn, starting with copy and paste. First you will make a copy of the first slide at the end of the presentation.

1.   Select the first slide, if it is not already selected, by clicking on the slide icon next to the number **1**.

2.   Click on the **Copy** icon 🖳, or select **Edit, Copy** to copy the slide into the computer's clipboard.

3.   Select the third slide by clicking on the slide icon next to the number **3**.

4.   Click on the **Paste** icon 🖳, or select **Edit, Paste**. A second copy of slide 1 will appear as a new slide 4.

Q3   How would you move a slide using the Edit commands?

Now you will delete the slide you just copied, in the same way that you deleted slides from presentations in Chapter 15.

5.   Select slide **4** by clicking on the slide icon next to the number 4.

6.   Press the **Delete** key on the keyboard, or select **Edit, Delete Slide**.

It is sometimes quicker to move or copy slides using drag and drop. The steps below show how to move the second slide below the third one in this way. The method for copying slides is the same except that you must hold down the key marked **Ctrl** while dragging.

7.   Click on the slide icon ⬚ next to the number **2** on the second slide to select the slide. All the text from the slide will be highlighted.

8.   Hold down the mouse button and drag the mouse pointer downwards. A horizontal line will appear on the screen. Drag the line down below the words Postgraduate Opportunities and release the mouse button.

Slides 2 and 3 should now have swapped places on the presentation. If you made a mistake when you were dragging the slide you can undo it either by selecting **Edit, Undo** or clicking on the **Undo** button ↰.

The third way to move slides is to use the Outlining toolbar on the left of the screen. The relevant buttons are described below.

- ⬆ *Move Up* This button moves a slide up one position.
- ⬇ *Move Down* This button moves a slide down one position.
- ⬆ *Collapse All* Shows only the slide titles.
- ⬇ *Expand All* Shows the whole slide.

▣ **Version 7**   The Expand All and Collapse All buttons are called Show All and Show Titles.

The Expand and Collapse buttons are particularly useful for long presentations like the ones created in Chapter 15. You will try them out now in conjunction with the Move buttons, but you do not always have to collapse the slides in order to move them. You will use these buttons to put back the slide you just moved.

9.   Click on the **Collapse All** button to display only the slide titles, then select slide **3** if it is not still selected and click on the **Move Up** button.

The slide will move back to its original position.

10. Click on the **Expand All** button to see the whole slides again in the new order.

16.6   Inserting a new slide

You will now insert a new slide in between the second and third. The new slide will contain a picture as well as text. The easiest way to create a slide containing a picture is to choose the appropriate layout by following the steps below, and then edit the slide in Slide view.

1. Select slide number **2**, then click the **Slide View** icon.

2. Click on the **New Slide** icon or select **Insert, New Slide**. The New Slide dialogue box shown previously in Figure 16.1 will appear again.

3. Select the layout in the bottom left corner, and click on **OK**. You will see the screen shown in Figure 16.7.

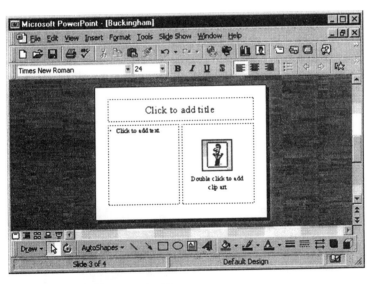

Figure 16.7 Blank slide with AutoLayout

16.7 Editing slides in slide view

The blank slide you have created contains three areas for adding information. The top box will hold the title, the box on the left will hold the bulleted list and the box on the right will hold the picture. The slide you will now create is shown in Figure 16.8.

1. Click on the box marked **Click to add title** and type the text **Campus**.

2. Click on the box marked **Click to add text** and type the text **Hunter Street**, then press **Enter**.

3. Type in the remaining two headings shown in Figure 16.8: **Chandos Road** and **Verney Park**.

4. Double click on the box marked **Double click to add clip art**, and you may see a message reminding you that further clips are available on CD-ROM. If this message appears, click on **OK** and you will see the screen in Figure 16.9.

Q4   Which category would you choose to find a picture of a lion?

5. Select the category **Academic**.

6. Click on the picture shown in Figure 16.8, then click on **Insert**. The image will appear on your slide with selection handles round it, and can be dragged to any desired position.

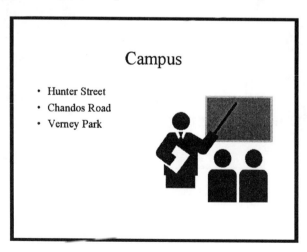

Figure 16.8 Slide with images and text

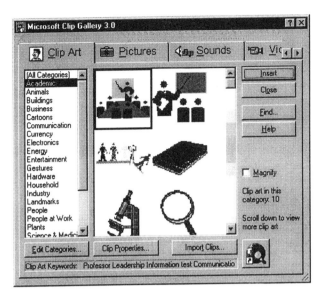

Figure 16.9 Microsoft Clip Art Gallery

The slide is now complete. If you ever wish to create a slide with a layout that is different from all of those shown in the New Slide dialogue box of Figure 16.1, then you should select the blank layout in the bottom right corner. Pictures and text can then be added to the slide using the tools on the drawing toolbar.

16.8 Using the drawing toolbar

You will now use the drawing toolbar to add some shapes to your presentation. You will then animate the drawings using the animation effects feature. The slide you will create is shown in Figure 16.10.

1. Stay in Slide view and click on the **New Slide** icon or select **Insert, New Slide.** The New Slide dialogue box shown previously in Figure 16.1 will appear again.

2. Select the layout on the bottom row, second from the right and click on **OK.**

3. Click on the text **Click to add title** and type the title line **Watch these drawings**.

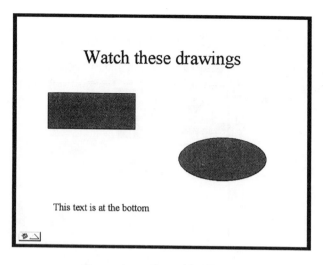

Figure 16.10 Slide with drawings

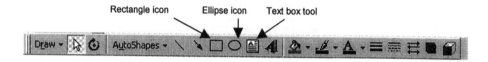

Rectangle icon   Ellipse icon   Text box tool

Figure 16.11 Drawing toolbar

Version 7 The toolbar is slightly different and may appear down the left side of the screen.

4. Click on the **Rectangle Tool** icon on the drawing toolbar shown in Figure 16.11 to switch on the rectangle tool.

5. Move the mouse pointer up so that it is just below the title line, then **click and drag** the mouse down and to the right, to draw a rectangle like that shown in Figure 16.10.

6. Click on the **Ellipse Tool** icon on the drawing toolbar shown in Figure 16.11 to switch on the ellipse tool.

7. Move the mouse pointer up so that it is just below the rectangle and to the right of it, then **click and drag** the mouse down and to the right, to draw an ellipse like that shown in Figure 16.10.

8. Click on the **Text Box Tool** icon on the drawing toolbar shown in Figure 16.11 to switch on the text box tool.

9.   Move the mouse pointer up so that it is below the rectangle and ellipse you have already drawn, then **click and drag** the mouse down and to the right, to draw a text box. Type the text **This text is at the bottom** into the text box so that the slide looks similar to that in Figure 16.10.

16.9   Animate the drawings

You will now add various animation effects to the slide you have just created.

1.   Select the **ellipse**, then click the **Animation Effects** icon 🌟 on the toolbar and you will see the Animation Effects shown in Figure 16.12.

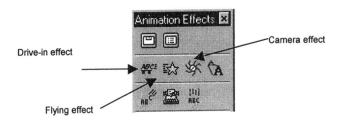

Figure 16.12 Animation Effects

2.   Select the **Flying Effect** icon, and check that the **Animation Order** box is set to **1**.

3.   Select the **rectangle**, then click the **Camera Effect** icon 🌟, and check that the **Animation Order** box is set to **2**.

4.   Select the text: **This text is at the bottom** and notice that the icons in the Animation Effects box change.

5.   Click the **Typewriter Text Effect** icon, 🖿 and check that the **Animation Order** box is set to **3**.

6.   **Close** ✕ the **Animation Effects** box.

7.   Switch to **Slide Show** view, and the slide will appear with just the title line showing. Click on the **left mouse** button to see each of the three animated items appear, then **exit** from Slide Show view.

16.10   Sharing data between applications

The simplest way to share data between two applications is to select the data in one application, then cut or copy it and paste it into the other application. This technique has a variety of uses. For example, it could be used to copy tables and charts from Excel spreadsheets into other Office applications such as Word or Access, or to copy text from Word documents back into Excel. You will use it now to copy the contents of one of the slides in your PowerPoint presentation into a Word document.

1. Click on the **Outline View** button or select **View, Outline** to switch back to Outline view.

2. Click on the slide icon next to the number **2** on the second slide to select the slide. All the text from the slide will be highlighted.

3. Click on the **Copy** icon , or select **Edit, Copy** to copy the slide into the clipboard.

4. Click on the **Minimise** button on the PowerPoint window to hide the PowerPoint screen.

5. Start up **Microsoft Word** and create a **New Document**.

6. Click on the **Paste** icon, or select **Edit, Paste**. All the text from the PowerPoint slide will appear in the Word document.

An alternative way to copy and move data between applications is to rearrange the application windows so that they can be viewed simultaneously, and then drag and drop the data between the windows. Both methods have the same effect, so the choice is purely a matter of taste.

16.11   Closing down the applications

1. Click on the **Close** button in the Microsoft Word window to close Word. There is no need to save the changes to the document.

2. Click on the words **Microsoft PowerPoint** in the taskbar at the bottom of the computer screen. This will restore the PowerPoint screen.

3.   Click on the **Close** ![X] button in the inner PowerPoint window to close the Buckingham presentation. Click on **Yes** when you are asked whether you would like to save the changes to the Buckingham presentation. Then click on the main **Close** ![X] button to close PowerPoint.

16.12 Summary

In this chapter you have been shown the following:

- The easiest way to add text to a blank presentation is to use **Outline** view.
- There are three ways to move slides within a presentation: **cut** and **paste**, **drag** and **drop** and the **Move** buttons on the toolbar.
- Data can also be moved between different applications using cut and paste and drag and drop.
- Drag and drop can also be used to copy data, by holding down the **Ctrl** key when dragging.
- Drawings can be added using the **Drawing** toolbar
- Animation can be added by using the **Animation Effects** icon.

16.13 Written exercises

16.13.1   Describe the purpose of each of the buttons on the Outlining toolbar in your own words.

16.13.2   Explain how you would copy a chart from Excel into Word.

16.14 Practical exercises

16.14.1   Create a presentation on a subject of your choice, starting from a Blank Presentation. Use a different Autolayout from those used in this chapter, and include at least four slides in the presentation. Insert an additional slide somewhere in the middle of the presentation, with a different AutoLayout from the main presentation. Include at least one picture from the ClipArt Gallery.

16.14.2   a) Start up Excel and create a small table of data.

b) Copy the data into a Word document.
c) Go back to Excel and create a chart based on your data.
d) Copy the chart into the Word document.
e) Type some text in the Word document, and copy it back into the Excel file.

Excel Functions

A.1 Math

ABS	Returns the absolute value of a number
ACOS	Returns the arccosine of a number
ACOSH	Returns the inverse hyperbolic cosine of a number
ASIN	Returns the arcsine of a number
ASINH	Returns the inverse hyperbolic sine of a number
ATAN	Returns the arctangent of a number
ATAN2	Returns the arctangent from x- and y- coordinates
ATANH	Returns the inverse hyperbolic tangent of a number
CEILING	Rounds a number to the nearest integer or to the nearest multiple of significance
COMBIN	Returns the number of combinations for a given number of objects
COS	Returns the cosine of a number
COSH	Returns the hyperbolic cosine of a number
COUNTIF	Counts the number of non-blank cells within a range which meet the given criteria
DEGREES	Converts radians to degrees
EVEN	Rounds a number up to the nearest even integer
EXP	Returns e raised to the power of a given number
FACT	Returns the factorial of a number
FACTDOUBLE	Returns the double factorial of a number
FLOOR	Rounds a number down, toward zero
GCD	Returns the greatest common divisor
INT	Rounds a number down to the nearest integer
LCM	Returns the least common multiple
LN	Returns the natural logarithm of a number
LOG	Returns the logarithm of a number to a specified base
LOG10	Returns the base-10 logarithm of a number
MDETERM	Returns the matrix determinant of an array
MINVERSE	Returns the matrix inverse of an array
MMULT	Returns the matrix product of two arrays
MOD	Returns the remainder from division
MROUND	Returns a number rounded to the desired multiple
MULTINOMIAL	Returns the multinomial of a set of numbers
ODD	Rounds a number up to the nearest odd integer
PI	Returns the value of Pi
POWER	Returns the result of a number raised to a power
PRODUCT	Multiplies its arguments

QUOTIENT	Returns the integer portion of a division
RADIANS	Converts degrees to radians
RAND	Returns a random number between 0 and 1
RANDBETWEEN	
	Returns a random number between the numbers you specify
ROMAN	Converts an Arabic numeral to Roman, as text
ROUND	Rounds a number to a specified number of digits
ROUNDDOWN	Rounds a number down, toward zero
ROUNDUP	Rounds a number up, away from zero
SERIESSUM	Returns the sum of a power series based on the formula
SIGN	Returns the sign of a number
SIN	Returns the sine of the given angle
SINH	Returns the hyperbolic sine of a number
SQRT	Returns a positive square root
SQRTPI	Returns the square root of (number * PI)
SUM	Adds its arguments
SUMIF	Adds the cells specified by a given criteria
SUMPRODUCT	Returns the sum of the products of corresponding array components
SUMSQ	Returns the sum of the squares of the arguments
SUMX2MY2	Returns the sum of the difference of squares of corresponding values in two arrays
SUMX2PY2	Returns the sum of the sum of squares of corresponding values in two arrays
SUMXMY2	Returns the sum of squares of differences of corresponding values in two arrays
TAN	Returns the tangent of a number
TANH	Returns the hyperbolic tangent of a number
TRUNC	Truncates a number to an integer

A.2   Database and list management

DAVERAGE	Returns the average of selected database entries
DCOUNT	Counts the cells containing numbers from a specified database and criteria
DCOUNTA	Counts nonblank cells from a specified database and criteria
DGET	Extracts from a database a single record that matches the specified criteria
DMAX	Returns the maximum value from selected database entries
DMIN	Returns the minimum value from selected database entries
DPRODUCT	Multiplies the values in a particular field of records that match the criteria in a database
DSTDEV	Estimates the standard deviation based on a sample of selected database entries
DSTDEVP	Calculates the standard deviation based on the entire population of selected database entries

DSUM	Adds the numbers in the field column of records in the database that match the criteria
DVAR	Estimates variance based on a sample from selected database entries
DVARP	Calculates variance based on the entire population of selected database entries
SQLREQUEST	Connects with an external data source and runs a query from a worksheet, then returns the result as an array without the need for macro programming
SUBTOTAL	Returns a subtotal in a list or list or database

A.3　Date and time

DATE	Returns the serial number of a particular date
DATEVALUE	Converts a date in the form of text to a serial number
DAY	Converts a serial number to a day of the month
DAYS360	Calculates the number of days between two dates based on a 360-day year
EDATE	Returns the serial number of the date that is the indicated number of months before or after the start date
EOMONTH	Returns the serial number of the last day of the month before or after a specified number of months
HOUR	Converts a serial number to an hour
MINUTE	Converts a serial number to a minute
MONTH	Converts a serial number to a month
NETWORKDAYS	
	Returns the number of whole workdays between two dates
NOW	Returns the serial number of the current date and time
SECOND	Converts a serial number to a second
TIME	Returns the serial number of a particular time
TIMEVALUE	Converts a time in the form of text to a serial number
TODAY	Returns the serial number of today's date
WEEKDAY	Converts a serial number to a day of the week
WORKDAY	Returns the serial number of the date before or after a specified number of workdays
YEAR	Converts a serial number to a year
YEARFRAC	Returns the year fraction representing the number of whole days between start_date and end_date

A.4　Engineering

BESSELI	Returns the modified Bessel function In(x)
BESSELJ	Returns the Bessel function Jn(x)

BESSELK	Returns the modified Bessel function Kn(x)
BESSELY	Returns the Bessel function Yn(x)
BIN2DEC	Converts a binary number to decimal
BIN2HEX	Converts a binary number to hexadecimal
BIN2OCT	Converts a binary number to octal
COMPLEX	Converts real and imaginary coefficients into a complex number
CONVERT	Converts a number from one measurement system to another
DEC2BIN	Converts a decimal number to binary
DEC2HEX	Converts a decimal number to hexadecimal
DEC2OCT	Converts a decimal number to octal
DELTA	Tests whether two values are equal
ERF	Returns the error function
ERFC	Returns the complementary error function
GESTEP	Tests whether a number is greater than a threshold value
HEX2BIN	Converts a hexadecimal number to binary
HEX2DEC	Converts a hexadecimal number to decimal
HEX2OCT	Converts a hexadecimal number to octal
IMABS	Returns the absolute value (modulus) of a complex number
IMAGINARY	Returns the imaginary coefficient of a complex number
IMARGUMENT	Returns the argument theta, an angle expressed in radians
IMCONJUGATE	Returns the complex conjugate of a complex number
IMCOS	Returns the cosine of a complex number
IMDIV	Returns the quotient of two complex numbers
IMEXP	Returns the exponential of a complex number
IMLN	Returns the natural logarithm of a complex number
IMLOG10	Returns the base-10 logarithm of a complex number
IMLOG2	Returns the base-2 logarithm of a complex number
IMPOWER	Returns a complex number raised to an integer power
IMPRODUCT	Returns the product of two complex numbers
IMREAL	Returns the real coefficient of a complex number
IMSIN	Returns the sine of a complex number
IMSQRT	Returns the square root of a complex number
IMSUB	Returns the difference of two complex numbers
IMSUM	Returns the sum of complex numbers
OCT2BIN	Converts an octal number to binary
OCT2DEC	Converts an octal number to decimal
OCT2HEX	Converts an octal number to hexadecimal
SQRTPI	Returns the square root of (number * PI)

A.5   Financial

ACCRINT	Returns the accrued interest for a security that pays periodic interest
ACCRINTM	Returns the accrued interest for a security that pays interest at maturity
AMORDEGRC	Returns the depreciation for each accounting period

AMORLINC	Returns the depreciation for each accounting period
COUPDAYBS	Returns the number of days from the beginning of the coupon period to the settlement date
COUPDAYS	Returns the number of days in the coupon period that contains the settlement date
COUPDAYSNC	Returns the number of days from the settlement date to the next coupon date
COUPNCD	Returns the next coupon date after the settlement date
COUPNUM	Returns the number of coupons payable between the settlement date and maturity date
COUPPCD	Returns the previous coupon date before the settlement date
CUMIPMT	Returns the cumulative interest paid between two periods
CUMPRINC	Returns the cumulative principal paid on a loan between two periods
DB	Returns the depreciation of an asset for a specified period using the fixed-declining balance method
DDB	Returns the depreciation of an asset for a spcified period using the double-declining balance method or some other method you specify
DISC	Returns the discount rate for a security
DURATION	Returns the annual duration of a security with periodic interest payments
EFFECT	Returns the effective annual interest rate
FV	Returns the future value of an investment
FVSCHEDULE	Returns the future value of an initial principal after applying a series of compound interest rates
INTRATE	Returns the interest rate for a fully invested security
IPMT	Returns the interest payment for an investment for a given period
IRR	Returns the internal rate of return for a series of cash flows
MIRR	Returns the internal rate of return where positive and negative cash flows are financed at different rates
NOMINAL	Returns the annual nominal interest rate
NPER	Returns the number of periods for an investment
NPV	Returns the net present value of an investment based on a series of periodic cash flows and a discount rate
ODDFYIELD	Returns the yield of a security with an odd first period
ODDLYIELD	Returns the yield of a security with an odd last period
PMT	Returns the periodic payment for an annuity
PPMT	Returns the payment on the principal for an investment for a given period
PV	Returns the present value of an investment
RATE	Returns the interest rate per period of an annuity
RECEIVED	Returns the amount received at maturity for a fully invested security
SLN	Returns the straight-line depreciation of an asset for one period
SYD	Returns the sum-of-years' digits depreciation of an asset for a specified period
TBILLYIELD	Returns the yield for a Treasury bill
VDB	Returns the depreciation of an asset for a specified or partial period using a declining balance method

XIRR	Returns the internal rate of return for a schedule of cash flows that is not necessarily periodic
XNPV	Returns the net present value for a schedule of cash flows that is not necessarily periodic
YIELD	Returns the yield on a security that pays periodic interest
YIELDDISC	Returns the annual yield for a discounted security. For example, a treasury bill
YIELDMAT	Returns the annual yield of a security that pays interest at maturity

A.6   Information

CELL	Returns information about the formatting, location, or contents of a cell
COUNTBLANK	Counts the number of blank cells within a range
ERROR.TYPE	Returns a number corresponding to an error type
INFO	Returns information about the current operating environment
ISBLANK	Returns TRUE if the value is blank
ISERR	Returns TRUE if the value is any error value except #N/A
ISERROR	Returns TRUE if the value is any error value
ISEVEN	Returns TRUE if the number is even
ISLOGICAL	Returns TRUE if the value is a logical value
ISNA	Returns TRUE if the value is the #N/A error value
ISNONTEXT	Returns TRUE if the value is not text
ISNUMBER	Returns TRUE if the value is a number
ISODD	Returns TRUE if the number is odd
ISREF	Returns TRUE if the value is a reference
ISTEXT	Returns TRUE if the value is text
N	Returns a value converted to a number
NA	Returns the error value #N/A
TYPE	Returns a number indicating the data type of a value

A.7   Logical

AND	Returns TRUE if all its arguments are TRUE
FALSE	Returns the logical value FALSE
IF	Specifies a logical test to perform
NOT	Reverses the logic of its argument
OR	Returns TRUE if any argument is TRUE
TRUE	Returns the logical value TRUE

ADDRESS	Returns a reference as text to a single cell in a worksheet
AREAS	Returns the number of areas in a reference
CHOOSE	Chooses a value from a list of values
COLUMN	Returns the column number of a reference
COLUMNS	Returns the number of columns in a reference
HLOOKUP	Looks in the top row of an array and returns the value of the indicated cell
INDEX	Uses an index to choose a value from a reference or array
INDIRECT	Returns a reference indicated by a text value
LOOKUP	Looks up values in a vector or array
MATCH	Looks up values in a reference or array
OFFSET	Returns a reference offset from a given reference
ROW	Returns the row number of a reference
ROWS	Returns the number of rows in a reference
TRANSPOSE	Returns the transpose of an array
VLOOKUP	Looks in the first column of an array and moves across the row to return the value of a cell

A.9   Statistical

AVEDEV	Returns the average of the absolute deviations of data points from their mean
AVERAGE	Returns the average of its arguments
BETADIST	Returns the cumulative beta probability density function
BETAINV	Returns the inverse of the cumulative beta probability density function
BINOMDIST	Returns the individual term binomial distribution probability
CHIDIST	Returns the one-tailed probability of the chi-squared distribution
CHIINV	Returns the inverse of the one-tailed probability of the chi-squared distribution
CHITEST	Returns the test for independence
CONFIDENCE	Returns the confidence interval for a population mean
CORREL	Returns the correlation coefficient between two data sets
COUNT	Counts how many numbers are in the list of arguments
COUNTA	Counts how many values are in the list of arguments
COVAR	Returns covariance, the average of the products of paired deviations
CRITBINOM	Returns the smallest value for which the cumulative binomial distribution is less than or equal to a criterion value
DEVSQ	Returns the sum of squares of deviations
EXPONDIST	Returns the exponential distribution
FDIST	Returns the F probability distribution
FINV	Returns the inverse of the F probability distribution

FISHER	Returns the Fisher transformation
FISHERINV	Returns the inverse of the Fisher transformation
FORECAST	Returns a value along a linear trend
FREQUENCY	Returns a frequency distribution as a vertical array
FTEST	Returns the result of an F-test
GAMMADIST	Returns the gamma distribution
GAMMAINV	Returns the inverse of the gamma cumulative distribution
GAMMALN	Returns the natural logarithm of the gamma function, $G(x)$
GEOMEAN	Returns the geometric mean
GROWTH	Returns values along an exponential trend
HARMEAN	Returns the harmonic mean
HYPGEOMDIST	Returns the hypergeometric distribution
INTERCEPT	Returns the intercept of the linear regression line
KURT	Returns the kurtosis of a data set
LARGE	Returns the k-th largest value in a data set
LINEST	Returns the parameters of a linear trend
LOGEST	Returns the parameters of an exponential trend
LOGINV	Returns the inverse of the lognormal distribution
LOGNORMDIST	
	Returns the cumulative lognormal distribution
MAX	Returns the maximum value in a list of arguments
MEDIAN	Returns the median of the given numbers
MIN	Returns the minimum value in a list of arguments
MODE	Returns the most common value in a data set
NEGBINOMDIST	
	Returns the negative binomial distribution
NORMDIST	Returns the normal cumulative distribution
NORMINV	Returns the inverse of the normal cumulative distribution
NORMSDIST	Returns the standard normal cumulative distribution
NORMSINV	Returns the inverse of the standard normal cumulative distribution
PEARSON	Returns the Pearson product moment correlation coefficient
PERCENTILE	Returns the k-th percentile of values in a range
PERCENTRANK	
	Returns the percentage rank of a value in a data set
PERMUT	Returns the number of permutations for a given number of objects
POISSON	Returns the Poisson distribution
PROB	Returns the probability that values in a range are between two limits
QUARTILE	Returns the quartile of a data set
RANK	Returns the rank of a number in a list of numbers
RSQ	Returns the square of the Pearson product moment correlatin coefficient
SKEW	Returns the skewness of a distribution
SLOPE	Returns the slope of the linear regression line
SMALL	Returns the k-th smallest value in a data set
STANDARDIZE	Returns a normalized value
STDEV	Estimates standard deviation based on a sample
STDEVP	Calculates standard deviation based on the entire population

STEYX	Returns the standard error of the predicted y-value for each x in the regression
TDIST	Returns the Student's t-distribution
TINV	Returns the inverse of the Student's t-distribution
TREND	Returns values along a linear trend
TRIMMEAN	Returns the mean of the interior of a data set
TTEST	Returns the probability associated with a Student's t-Test
VAR	Estimates variance based on a sample
VARP	Calculates variance based on the entire population
WEIBULL	Returns the Weibull distribution
ZTEST	Returns the two-tailed P-value of a z-test

A.10 Text

CHAR	Returns the character specified by the code number
CLEAN	Removes all nonprintable characters from text
CODE	Returns a numeric code for the first character in a text string
CONCATENATE	
	Joins several text items into one text item
DOLLAR	Converts a number to text, using currency format
EXACT	Checks to see if two text values are identical
FIND	Finds one text value within another (case-sensitive)
FIXED	Formats a number as text with a fixed number of decimals
LEFT	Returns the leftmost characters from a text value
LEN	Returns the number of characters in a text string
LOWER	Converts text to lowercase
MID	Returns a specific number of characters from a text string starting at the position you specify
PROPER	Capitalizes the first letter in each word of a text value
REPLACE	Replaces characters within text
REPT	Repeats text a given number of times
RIGHT	Returns the rightmost characters from a text value
SEARCH	Finds one text value within another (not case-sensitive)
SUBSTITUTE	Substitutes new text for old text in a text string
T	Converts its arguments to text
TEXT	Formats a number and converts it to text
TRIM	Removes spaces from text
UPPER	Converts text to uppercase
VALUE	Converts a text argument to a number

Index

A

Absolute cell address, 89, 90, 97–99, 102
Access
    changing table structure, 143
    closing a database, 118, 129
    creating a database, 121
    creating a new table, 151
    creating a table, 118, 122, 138
    data entry, 144
    entering data, 118, 126, 186, 189
    filtering a database, 128
    modifying field properties, 136
    opening a database, 134
    saving a table, 142
    sorting data, 127
    starting, 119
    viewing table design, 135
Aligned headings, 40
Aligning text, 39
Alignment, 39, 47, 82
    centre, 81
Amending chart features, 107
Animation, 201, 212–214, 216, 225, 227, 229
Answer Wizard, 11, 65
AutoContent Wizard, 202, 204, 205, 211, 214, 215
AutoForm, 184, 185, 187, 198
Autoformat, 74, 84, 86–88
AutoNumber, 126, 133, 137, 139, 140, 146, 147, 156
Autosum, 96, 97, 99, 101

B

Backspace, 25
Bold, 82
Bookman Old Style, 37
Bullet points, 35, 43, 44, 48, 49, 212, 213, 220

C

Cancel, 4, 11, 12, 29, 45, 120, 202, 217
Caption, 137, 138
CD-ROM, 224
Cell address, 63, 89, 91, 94, 97, 102, 112
Chart
    gridlines, 85, 86, 105, 108
    location, 106
    major gridlines, 105, 108
    multi-series, 102, 115, 116
    show data table, 105
    title, 104
    type, 103, 107
    wizard, 102–107, 109, 110, 115
    x-axis category, 108
    y-axis value, 104
Clipboard, 23, 24, 55, 78, 79, 221, 228
Close Button, 9, 64
Closing applications, 228
Column, 64, 67, 81, 83, 86, 103, 106, 116
Columnar, 184, 185
Contents and Index, 10, 11
Copy icon, 23, 79, 93, 110, 113, 221, 228
Courier New, 38
Creating a new workbook, 68
Criteria, 170–175
Currency, 82, 83, 86, 88, 97, 98, 112, 130, 133, 144, 146, 147
Current cell, 65
Current Worksheet, 65
Curriculum vitae, 34, 49
Cursor, 10
Custom header, 114, 115
Customer details, 122, 129, 199
Cut icon, 24, 33, 80, 145

D

Database, 1, 118–123, 126, 129, 130–135, 138, 139, 145–151, 154, 156, 159–165, 171, 175, 178–187, 191, 193, 197, 198, 199, 200, 206
Database management system, 119

Tabular, 184
Taskbar, 5, 6, 8, 9, 58, 110, 228
Template, 123, 201, 202, 204, 211–216
Temporary, 4, 7, 12, 14, 16, 69
Terminology, 3
Text blocks
   deleting, 25
   moving, 24
   selecting, 22
Tool Bar, 9
Transition effects, 212–214
Typewriter, 7, 227

U

Underline, 36–38, 49, 76, 77, 87
Undo clear, 26
Undo command, 26, 32
Unfreeze panes, 98, 99

Up scroll arrow, 41, 45
User name, 3, 4
Using help, 10, 65

W

Windows 95, 1, 2, 3, 52
Wizard, 102, 107, 122, 123, 125, 132,
   138, 184, 187, 193, 202, 204
Word processor, 1, 7, 8, 13, 14, 22, 27
Word screen displays
   master document, 31
   normal, 31, 34, 38
   outline, 31, 34, 205, 208, 210–212,
     214, 216, 218–221, 228, 229
   page layout, 31, 34, 44, 46
Workbook, 62, 63, 68, 71–73, 75
Worksheet, 2, 62, 63, 66, 67, 72, 74, 114